Spanish Festivals and Traditions

Activities and Teaching Ideas for Primary Schools

Nicolette Hannam and Michelle Williams

Brilliant
PUBLICATIONS

Dedication
In memory of my lovely mum, Pauline Cranfield.
Michelle Williams.

We hope you and your pupils enjoy learning about the festivals and traditions in this book. Brilliant Publications publishes many other books for teaching modern foreign languages. To find out more details on any of the titles listed below, please log onto our website: www.brilliantpublications.co.uk.

100+ Fun Ideas for Practising Modern Foreign Languages in the Primary Classroom	978-1-903853-98-6
More Fun Ideas for Advancing Modern Foreign Languages in the Primary Classroom	978-1-905780-72-3
¡Es Español!	978-1-903853-64-1
Juguemos Todos Juntos	978-1-903853-95-5
¡Vamos a Cantar!	978-1-905780-13-6
Spanish Pen Pals Made Easy	978-1-905780-42-3
Lotto en Español	978-1-905780-47-1
Buena Idea	978-1-905780-63-1
Chantez Plus Fort!	978-1-903853-37-5
Hexagonie 1	978-1-905780-59-4
Hexagonie 2	978-1-905780-18-1
Jouons Tous Ensemble	978-1-903853-81-8
C'est Français!	978-1-903853-02-3
J'aime Chanter!	978-1-905780-11-2
J'aime Parler!	978-1-905780-12-9
French Pen Pals Made Easy	978-1-905780-10-5
Loto Français	978-1-905780-45-7
French Festivals and Traditions	978-1-905780-44-0
Bonne Idée	978-1-905780-62-4
Unforgettable French	978-1-905780-54-9
Das ist Deutsch	978-1-905780-15-0
Wir Spielen Zusammen	978-1-903853-97-9
German Pen Pals Made Easy	978-1-905780-43-3
Deutsch-Lotto	978-1-905780-46-4
German Festivals and Traditions	978-1-905780-52-5
Gute Idee	978-1-905780-65-5
Giochiamo Tutti Insieme	978-1-903853-96-2
Lotto in Italiano	978-1-905780-48-8
Buon'Idea	978-1-905780-64-8

Published by Brilliant Publications
Unit 10
Sparrow Hall Farm
Edlesborough
Dunstable
Bedfordshire
LU6 2ES, UK

Website: www.brilliantpublications.co.uk

General information enquiries:
Tel: 01525 222292

The name Brilliant Publications and the logo are registered trademarks.

Written by Nicolette Hannam and Michelle Williams
Illustrated by Kerry Ingham
Front cover designed by Brilliant Publications

© Text Nicolette Hannam and Michelle Williams 2009
© Design Brilliant Publications 2009

Printed ISBN: 978-1-905780-53-2
ebook ISBN: 978-0-85747-004-1

First printed and published in the UK in 2010

The right of Nicolette Hannam and Michelle Williams to be identified as the authors of this work has been asserted by themselves in accordance with the Copyright, Designs and Patents Act 1988.

Pages 10–12, 15, 17–18, 21, 24, 27–28, 31, 33, 35, 37, 39, 43, 46, 51, 55–56, 58, 62, 64, 66, 70, 72, 74, 77, 79, 83–84, 87–88, and 91–104 may be photocopied by individual teachers acting on behalf of the purchasing institution for classroom use only, without permission from the publisher and without declaration to the Publishers Licensing Society. The materials may not be reproduced in any other form or for any other purpose without the prior permission of the publisher.

The authors and publishers would like to thank Belén de Vicente Fisher for her detailed and helpful comments on the manuscript.

Contents

Month	Mes	Festival/Tradition
January	enero	¡Año Nuevo!/El día de los Reyes (New Year's Day/Epiphany) 8
February	febrero	Carnaval (Festival time) 13
		El día de San Valentín (Valentine's Day) 16
March	marzo	Las Fallas de San José (The Torches of Saint Joseph) 19
		El Festival de Flamenco de Jerez (Jerez Flamenco Festival) 22
April	abril	Semana Santa (Holy Week, Easter) 25
		La Feria de abril (Seville's April Fair) 29
May	mayo	Las Cruces de mayo (May Crosses) 32
		La Feria del Caballo (Jerez Horse Fair) 34
		El día de la Madre (Mother's Day) 36
June	junio	Las Hogueras de San Juan (Bonfires of Saint John) 38
		Feliz Cumpleaños (Happy Birthday) 40
July	julio	Las Fiestas de San Fermín 44
		Symbols of Spain 47
		Cuentos de hadas (Fairy stories) 52
August	agosto	La Tomatina (The world's biggest food fight) 57
		Planning a holiday 59
		How is Spanish culture incorporated into our everyday life? 63
September	septiembre	La Fiesta de la Vendimia (Grape harvest festival) 65
		La Vuelta ciclista a España (Annual cycle race) 67
		A typical school day in Spain 68
		Comparing pastimes and everyday life 71
October	octubre	El día de la Hispanidad (Spanish National Day) 73
		Halloween 75
		Challenging stereotypes 78
		Role models for children 80
November	noviembre	Alimento español (Spanish Food) 81
		El día de Todos los Santos (All Saints Day) 85
		Comparing buildings and places 86
December	diciembre	Feliz Navidad (Happy Christmas) 89

Introduction

This book was written by a secondary and a primary school teacher to provide information about festivals and traditions in Spain.

Every month has ideas that support the intercultural strand of the *Framework for Modern Foreign Languages*. According to the *Framework,* by the end of Year 6 most children should be able to:

◆ Demonstrate understanding of and respect for cultural diversity.
◆ Present information about an aspect of another country.

The ideas in this book can be used to develop discussions about comparisons. The *Framework* suggests comparing attitudes towards aspects of everyday life (IU6.1) and understanding differences between people (IU6.2).

It then suggests children present information about an aspect of culture through a wide variety of media. By regularly using ideas from this book you are providing your pupils with a wealth of ideas.

Each month has a choice of guided sheets that can be photocopied. There is also a variety of suggested teaching activities, with vocabulary provided. Extension ideas are provided for more able pupils.

Running a Spanish Day (see Planning a Spanish Day for your school, pages 94–104) will complement your intercultural teaching and provide children with many opportunities to achieve a high standard in this area of Spanish. The Spanish vocabulary provided will support and reinforce your language work alongside this.

There are two analysis grids that show how and where the book covers the intercultural strand. The first (page 5) is split into year groups and shows where you can find work to cover the objectives for your own year group. The second grid (page 6) looks at each strand and shows where it is covered in the book. This will be extremely useful for MFL coordinators.

Spanish Festivals and Traditions
© *Nicolette Hannam, Michelle Williams and Brilliant Publications*

Analysis by year group

Year group	Objective	Covered in book
3	Identify other languages they'd like to learn	Planning a holiday (pages 59–62)
	Learn where Spanish is spoken	Planning a holiday (pages 59–62)
	Know some facts about one country	Throughout book
	Make contact with native speakers	Access contact through your Local Authority or the NACELL or CILT websites
	Compare different cultures	Throughout book: Feliz Cumpleaños (pages 40–43) A typical school day in Spain (pages 68–70) Comparing pastimes and everyday life (pages 71–72)
	Spanish song/rhyme	Feliz Navidad (pages 89–93)
4	Know about Spanish celebrations	Throughout book
	Identify similarities and differences in how festivals and special days are celebrated	El día de San Valentín (pages 16–18) Semana Santa (pages 25–28) Feliz Cumpleaños (pages 40–43) Feliz Navidad (pages 89–93)
	Use simple phrases to celebrate	Throughout book
	Compare everyday pastimes to their own	Comparing pastimes and everyday life (pages 71–72)
	Compare traditional stories	Cuentos de hadas (pages 52–56)
5	Compare particular aspects of everyday life to their own	A typical school day in Spain (pages 68–70) Alimento español (pages 81–84)
	Exchange information with a partner school	Access contact through your Local Authority or the NACELL or CILT websites
	Compare buildings and places in contrasting localities	Alimento español (pages 81–84)
	Investigate ways of travelling to another country/countries	Planning a holiday (pages 59–62)
	Consider how cultures of different countries are incorporated into everday life	A typical school day in Spain (pages 68–70) Comparing pastimes and everyday life (pages 71–72) How is Spanish culture incorporated into our everyday life? (pages 63–64)
	Compare symbols and products	Symbols of Spain (pages 47–51)
6	Understand and respect cultural diversity (different attitudes)	How is Spanish culture incorporated into our everyday life? (pages 63–64) – develop discussion from guided sheet (page 64)
	Recognize and challenge stereotypes	Challenging stereotypes (pages 78–79)
	Present information about an aspect of another country: – perform songs/plays/dramas – use ICT to present information – greater sense of audience	Year 6 pupils can choose one idea/topic from the book and use it to develop a PowerPoint presentation aimed at a given audience. Choose a specific festival from the book, eg Christmas or Easter, or they could do a geography presentation.

Analysis by objective

Learning objective		Covered in book
IU3.1	Learn about the different languages spoken by children in the school	Planning a holiday (pages 59–62). Could be developed from discussions around the Spanish language. Does anyone speak Spanish in our school? Which other languages are spoken? Why?
IU3.2	Locate country/countries where the language is spoken	Planning a holiday (pages 59–62)
IU3.3	Identify social conventions at home and in other cultures	Feliz Cumpleaños (pages 40–43) – typical names Social conventions addressed throughout book
IU3.4	Make direct or indirect contact with the country/countries where the language is spoken	We recommend that you approach your Local Authority for advice, or visit the NACELL or CILT websites
IU4.1	Learn about festivals and celebrations in different cultures	Throughout book
IU4.2	Know about some aspects of everyday life and compare them to their own	Throughout book, especially A typical school day in Spain (pages 68–70) and Comparing pastimes and everyday life (pages 71–72)
IU4.3	Compare traditional stories	Cuentos de hadas (pages 52–56)
IU4.4	Learn about ways of travelling to the country/countries	Planning a holiday (pages 59–62)
IU5.1	Look at further aspects of their everyday lives from the perspective of someone from another country	Guided sheet – What I know about Spain (page 88) See also, Spanish Day evaluation sheet (pages 103–104)
IU5.2	Recognize similarities and differences between places	Throughout book Planning a holiday (pages 59–62) – comparing two localities Alimento español (pages 81–84)
IU5.3	Compare symbols, objects or products which represent their own culture with those of another country	Symbols of Spain (pages 47–51) Alimento español (pages 81–84) Planning a holiday (pages 59–62) – develop locality discussion from guided sheet (page 62)
IU6.1	Compare attitudes towards aspects of everyday life	A typical school day in Spain (pages 68–70) Comparing pastimes and everyday life (pages 71–72) Role models for children (page 80) Alimento español (pages 81–84)
IU6.2	Recognize and understand some of the differences between people	Throughout book – comparing how people celebrate How is Spanish culture incorporated into our everyday life? (pages 63–64) – develop cultural diversity discussion from guided sheet (page 64) Challenging stereotypes (pages 78–79)
IU6.3	Present information about an aspect of culture	Children can be encouraged to develop plays, songs and dances from the information taught about Spanish culture They can use ICT (for example, PowerPoint) to present information for a given audience Can possibly be used for transition information/ assessment

Spanish Festivals and Traditions
© Nicolette Hannam, Michelle Williams and Brilliant Publications

Successful teaching ideas for new vocabulary

There are many ways to help children learn new vocabulary and it is important to use a variety of methods and make it fun. Below are some successful ideas that have been tried and tested:

♦ Very simply, hold up flashcards and ask the children to repeat the words after you. They like doing this in different voices.

♦ Mime a card. Children have to guess the word, in Spanish.

♦ Which flashcard am I holding? Hold flashcard facing you. Ask children to guess which one you are looking at. This tests memory and pronunciation.

♦ True or False. Children only repeat the flashcard after you if you are saying the word that matches it.

♦ Matching cards. Give out cards to match yours, for example with names of pets. Say a word and children hold up the matching card, if they have it.

♦ Children could sequence the words as you call them out.

♦ Children could stand in order with flashcards, for example, with names of the months. Or they could stand in alphabetical order.

♦ For colours, they could build towers in the order that you call out, using coloured bricks.

♦ Children could hold up key words as they hear them in a song.

♦ Children could draw what you say, using mini-whiteboards.

♦ Slap the flashcard! Or the correct part of a picture (for example, the face). Children come up to the board in pairs (boys versus girls is popular). They use their hands to touch (slap) the flashcard the teacher says. A point is given to the first one to touch the correct flashcard.

♦ Teach the children actions to go with the songs you learn.

♦ Use puppets or soft toys to ask and answer questions.

♦ Give the children cards with words and pictures and use them to play Pelmanism (also known as Pairs).

♦ As above, but play Snap.

♦ Picture lotto. Cross off pictures as you hear the word called out.

♦ Pictionary. The teacher can draw pictures, for example pets, and children call out as soon as they recognize it. Or they can play in small groups, on mini-whiteboards.

♦ Hangman (known as *El ahorcado* in Spanish).

♦ *Simon dice* (Simon says).

♦ Chinese Whispers.

♦ Kim's Game.

¡Año Nuevo!/El día de los Reyes

New Year's Day / Epiphany

Background information

In Spain, New Year's Day is spent quietly with family and friends after the celebrations from the night before. People wish each other *Feliz Año* or *Feliz Año Nuevo* (Happy New Year). Many families start the New Year with a winter breakfast of hot chocolate and fried pastries (*chocolate con churros*) to help them recover after the New Year's Eve parties!

El día de los Reyes (Epiphany) takes place on the 6th January. The date celebrating Christ's birth has changed throughout history. The 6th January was the day of celebration until the Roman church adopted the 25th December in the fourth century. Today the 6th January is known as Epiphany. In many parts of Europe the Christmas celebration, or the 'twelve days of Christmas', (between Christmas and the 6th January), does not end until this date, now considered to be when the Three Kings arrived in Bethlehem.

In Spain, tradition has it that the Three Kings, *los Reyes Magos*, are the ones who bring children their presents on the morning of the 6th January, or *el día de los Reyes*. Parents encourage their children to write to the Three Kings to ask for their presents, in the same way British children write to Father Christmas.

In some areas, children leave their shoes on the windowsill or balcony ready for their presents. Spanish children leave straw and carrots out for the Kings' camels and food and drink for the Kings! The Kings are called Melchor, Gaspar and Baltasar. Melchor brought gold for Jesus, Gaspar brought frankincense, and Baltasar brought myrrh.

In every town in Spain adults and children celebrate on the 6th January with parades and street parties to welcome the Three Kings. *La cabalgata de los Reyes Magos* (the parade of the Three Kings) is a big parade with large floats, each one decorated with a different theme. At the end of the procession come the Three Kings, each one in his own big carriage. People on the floats throw sweets for the children.

It is also tradition to have a special dessert called *Roscón de Reyes*, or Kings' Cake. This is a sweet cake in the shape of a ring, topped with crystalized fruit pieces. Sometimes it is served cut in half and filled with cream. A lucky charm is hidden inside the Kings' Cake. Traditionally the charm was a bean, but nowadays it is a ceramic figure. Although the cake has religious origins, it has become a tradition for families to gather together to cut the cake; whoever finds the bean will be crowned king or queen for the day.

In Spain, and other countries in the Catholic religion worldwide, the Twelfth Night and Epiphany mark the start of the Carnival season.

Teaching activities

◆ Explain to the children about the tradition of *Los Reyes.*

◆ Children could role play visiting their friends to wish them Happy New Year, *Feliz Año Nuevo.*

◆ Children mime making a Kings' Cake as you give instructions in Spanish (see recipe on page 10)

◆ You could make a Kings' cake and act out the tradition of eating *Roscón de Reyes.*

◆ Use a bean or a raisin instead of the lucky charm. You will need a crown for the top of the cake. Ask the children questions about the tradition of the cake, the taste and so on. This could all contribute to a display with photographs.

◆ Design your own recipe cards for making the Kings' Cake. Use a dictionary to draw and label the ingredients in Spanish.

◆ Role play buying the *Roscón de Reyes* in a Spanish bakery.

◆ Have a crown making competition, or design a charm.

◆ Discuss and compare how New Year is celebrated here and in Spain.

◆ Design a New Year's Day card. Include details of what will be studied throughout the year in Spanish lessons to inform parents.

◆ Use the Internet to research different festivals and traditions for New Year's Day in Spain and other countries.

◆ Children could use the guided sheet on page 11 to describe your New Year's traditions and celebrations to a real or imaginary Spanish friend.

◆ Use photocopiable sheet on page 12 to draw a picture of the Three Kings and their gifts. Melchor was an Arabian king who brought gold for Jesus. Gaspar brought frankincense and Baltasar brought myrrh.

◆ Can you set out any New Year's Resolutions for your class or your school?

Vocabulario

Feliz Año Nuevo!	Happy New Year!
Roscón de Reyes	A special 'King's Cake'
un amuleto	a charm
un rey	a king
una reina	a queen
una panadería	a bakery
una corona	a crown
harina	flour
azúcar	sugar
leche	milk
levedura	yeast
mantequilla	butter
huevos	eggs
sal	salt
azúcar glas	icing sugar
zumo de naranja	orange juice

Roscón de Reyes

Ingredients

Cake
3 $\frac{1}{2}$ cups of plain flour
1 packet of active dry yeast
$\frac{2}{3}$ cup of milk
$\frac{1}{3}$ cup of butter
$\frac{1}{3}$ cup of sugar
$\frac{1}{2}$ tsp salt
2 eggs

Topping
1 cup of icing sugar
2 tsp of orange juice
mixed peel to decorate

Instructions

◆ In a large bowl, mix $1\frac{1}{2}$ cups of flour and the yeast.

◆ In a small pan, heat the milk, butter, sugar and salt until warm.

◆ Add to the flour mixture.

◆ Add eggs and beat mixture until it can be kneaded.

◆ Knead in the remaining flour and shape into a ball. Cover and leave in a warm place until it doubles in size (1–2 hours).

◆ Shape the dough into a long sausage and join the ends together to make a ring.

◆ Cover and leave to rise in a warm place (30–40 minutes).

◆ Bake at 350°F for 30 minutes. Leave to cool.

◆ Mixing icing sugar with orange juice and spread over cake.

◆ Sprinkle with mixed peel.

Ingredientes

Pastel
3 $\frac{1}{2}$ vasos de harina
1 paquete de levadura
$\frac{2}{3}$ vasos de leche
$\frac{1}{3}$ vaso de mantequilla
$\frac{1}{3}$ vaso de azúcar
$\frac{1}{2}$ cucharadita de sal
2 huevos

Decoración
1 vaso de azúcar glas
2 cucharaditas de zumo de naranja
la piel de limón y naranja

Instrucciones

◆ En un bol grande, mezclar $1\frac{1}{2}$ vasos de harina y la levadura

◆ En un sartén calentar la leche, la mantequilla, el azúcar y la sal.

◆ Añadir la harina con la levadura.

◆ Añadir los huevos y batir la mezcla hasta formar una masa.

◆ Añadir la harina sobrante y continuar con la masa para formar una bola. Cubrir y dejar la masa reposar en un lugar cálido, hasta elevarse al doble (1–2 horas).

◆ Formar la masa como una salchicha grande y juntar las puntas para formar un círculo.

◆ Cubrir y reposar en un lugar cálido (30–40 minutos).

◆ Poner dentro del horno a 350°F por 30 minutos. Dejar enfriar.

◆ Mezclar el azúcar glas con el zumo de naranja y untar en el roscón.

◆ Adornar con la piel de limón y naranja.

Spanish Festivals and Traditions
© Nicolette Hannam, Michelle Williams and Brilliant Publications

¡Año Nuevo!

Nombre: Fecha:

I can describe how I celebrate New Year.

Use the space below to write a letter in English to an imaginary Spanish pen friend. Introduce yourself and explain where you live. Describe how you celebrate New Year. What do you eat? What do you do? Who do you spend it with? Can you explain the reasons for any of your traditions?

Extension activity

Write some questions that you could ask a Spanish friend about New Year. Are there any other questions you would like to ask a Spanish friend about their life?

El día de los Reyes

Nombre: Fecha:

I understand how and why *El día de los Reyes* is celebrated in Spain.

Can you draw floats with the three kings on them? Label each one, and their gifts.

Can you draw the items that Spanish children leave out on the eve of 5th January? Include shoes on a windowsill, straw and carrots for the Kings' camels and wine and food for the Kings.

Extension activity
Use the Internet to find out more about *El día de los Reyes*.

Spanish Festivals and Traditions
© Nicolette Hannam, Michelle Williams and Brilliant Publications

Carnaval

Festival Time

Background information

Carnival is prevalent in Roman Catholic areas and signals the beginning of Lent. The word *carnaval* comes from the Latin 'take off the flesh' and it is a time when people would make the most of eating fatty foods before Lent began. In the UK, Pancake Day signals the start of Lent.

Cádiz is particularly famous for its *Carnaval* and plans begin for it months in advance. A major part of the *Carnaval* is a contest between choirs, usually shown on television. They also have parades with floats. Often politicians and celebrities are parodied by people in fancy dress. Confetti and sweets are thrown to children from the floats.

The country of Spain is famous for its fiestas and there are many celebrations throughout the year, celebrated in a carnival atmosphere. Food, drink, dancing, music, parades and fireworks are typical of the fiesta! Most fiestas originate from religion and often honour a patron saint. In addition to the religious festivals, each 'comunidad' has its own individual fiesta with its own unique traditions.

San Juan is a traditional summer fiesta, originating in Valencia but now celebrated in many other places in Spain, with bonfires and fireworks. In Algemesí they have a fiesta to see which team can form the highest human tower. The bull running of San Fermín is famous, and described in more detail on pages 44–45. Even the smallest Spanish villages have fiestas, and rumour has it that there is a fiesta somewhere in Spain on every day of the year.

Teaching activities

◆ Design your *Carnaval* costume. You could base it on a politician or a celebrity that you admire.

◆ Make an invitation to a *Carnaval* party, using the template below, or make up your own.

> *Querido*
>
> *Te invito a que asistas a la fiesta de disfraces.*
>
> *Lugar: Mi casa*
> *Fecha: el 24 de agosto*
> *Hora: las seis*

Vocabulario

un rey	a king
una reina	a queen
un baile de máscara	a masked ball
una máscara	a mask
una carroza	a float
un disfraz	a costume
un desfile	a parade
los fuegos artificiales	fireworks
Querido …	Dear (to a boy)
Querida …	Dear (to a girl)
Te invito a que asistas a la fiesta de disfraces	You are invited to a fancy dress party
mi casa	at my house
lugar	place
fecha	date
hora	time

◆ Use the Internet to compare the Cádiz *Carnaval* in Spain to the Notting Hill Carnival in London.

◆ Plan a carnival day for your school. What could people wear? What could they eat? How would you explain the religious reasons behind a carnival?

◆ Design a poster advertising the Cádiz *Carnaval*.

◆ Write an acrostic poem using the word *Carnaval* and give information about carnivals in Spain.

◆ Write a diary entry pretending that you have been to a carnival. Describe what you did, what you saw, how you felt, and so on.

Carnaval

Nombre: Fecha:

I learned about *Carnaval* and *Fiestas* in Spain.

Imagine you are in a town in Spain, celebrating Carnaval with your friends and family.

Draw and describe what you hear.

What is a fiesta? Use this box to draw and describe one.

Extension activities

◆ Can you compare and contrast how you celebrate Pancake Day?

◆ Write a letter to a real or imaginary Spanish person to tell them how you celebrate.

El día de San Valentín
Valentine's Day

Background information

This American custom has been adopted in Spain, as in many other countries. On Valentine's Day, husbands give their wives flowers (usually roses) and unmarried couples exchange gifts. Here is a Spanish Valentine's Day poem:

Nunca digas nunca	Never say never
Tampoco digas siempre	Never say forever
Pero dime que me amas	But tell me you love me
Como nunca y para siempre.	For forever.

Teaching activities

◆ Make a Valentine's Day card or poster. Write some words on the board to help:

Words for Valentine's Day cards

Mi amor/Mi vida	My love
Querido …	Dear … (boy)
Querida ...	Dear … (girl)
Cásate conmigo	Marry me
Saludos	Love from

◆ Make a 'Chatterbox' finger game (see page 17 for instructions).

Here are some suggestions for things that could be written inside:

Te quiero.	I love/like you.
No te quiero.	I don't love/like you.
¿Quieres salir conmigo?	Will you go out with me?
¿Quieres casarte conmigo?	Will you marry me?
¿Cómo te llamas?	What is your name?

◆ Pupils could use any Spanish vocabulary they have learned for the words on the outside flaps, eg colours, numbers etc.

◆ Children could use the guided sheet on page 18 to design a Valentine's Day card or poster using Spanish vocabulary.

◆ Research poems by Gloria Fuertes (1917-1998), a famous Spanish children's poet.

Vocabulario

el amor	love
la amistad	friendship
Te quiero	I love/like you
No te quiero	I don't love/like you
¿Quieres casarte conmigo?	Will you marry me?
Feliz día de San Valentín	Happy Valentine's Day
Querido…	dear … (boy)
Querida ...	dear (girl)
Saludos	love from
¿Quieres salir conmigo?	Will you go out with me?
¿Cóme te llamas?	What's your name?

Spanish Festivals and Traditions
© *Nicolette Hannam, Michelle Williams and Brilliant Publications*

A chatterbox game

How to make a chatterbox

1   Fold a square piece of paper in half vertically and horizontally, and then unfold.

2   Fold all four corners so they meet at the centre point. Turn the folded square over.

3   Fold all four new corners so they meet at the centre point.

4   Fold the top edge to meet the bottom edge, crease the fold and unfold again. Fold the right edge to meet the left one, crease and unfold.

5   Hold the chatterbox as shown. Slip the pointer finger and thumb from each hand under the square flaps at the back, pinching the folds.

6.   Practise opening and closing the 'mouth' of the chatterbox.

7   Write a word on each of the four corners. Open the chatterbox up and write other words on all eight triangles, or put coloured dots. Finally, lift up the flaps and write your chosen sentences underneath each triangle. You are now ready to play!

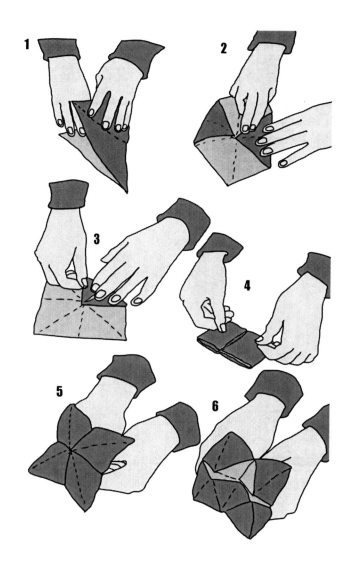

How to use a chatterbox

◆   Ask your friend to read each of the words displayed on the outside of the chatterbox and to choose one word. Spell out the word, using the Spanish alphabet, opening and closing the chatterbox as you say each letter.

◆   At the end of spelling this word, four of the inside words, or coloured dots, will be displayed. Ask your friend to read, or name, them and to choose one.

◆   Spell out that chosen word, opening and closing the 'bird's beak' again as you say each letter. At the end of this spelling, four of the inside words will be displayed. It may be the same four words or it may be the other four words.

◆   Ask your friend to read these four words and to choose one again. Open up the chosen flap.

◆   Read out the sentence under the flap and see how your partner responds!

El día de San Valentín

Nombre: Fecha:

I had fun learning about *El día de San Valentín*.

Design a Valentine's Day card or poster. Use some of the Spanish words we learnt.

Play with your Chatterbox with your friends. In this box write down the Spanish that you chose to use.

Extension activities

◆ Can you compare and contrast how you celebrate Valentine's Day?

◆ Write a letter to an imaginary or real Spanish person to tell them how you celebrate.

Spanish Festivals and Traditions
© Nicolette Hannam, Michelle Williams and Brilliant Publications

Las Fallas de San José

The Torches of Saint Joseph

Background information

This is a Valencian tradition in celebration of Saint Joseph and it is held on the 19th March each year. Huge papier-mâché models depicting local characters and politicians are created and set up in squares and streets all over Valencia. *Fallas* artists can spend up to a whole year designing and building these models. Each year there are competitions for the best *fallas* and the very best are kept for displays in a special museum in Valencia.

The celebrations last for 5 days and people dress up in regional costumes, medieval in style. They proudly wear expensive, traditional dress to show that they are from Valencia. Like many of the fiestas, there is music, dancing, processions, food, drink and fireworks. Paella originates in Valencia and is very popular.

Each day of *Fallas* begins at 8am with 'la despertá' or 'the wake up call'. Brass bands will play lively music through the streets, followed by people throwing firecrackers as they go. At 2pm there is 'mascletá' – an explosive display of firecrackers.

On the final night of *Fallas*, at around midnight, the models are set alight. The fires are known as 'Cremá'. One is selected to be the overall winner and is kept for inclusion in the museum. The final night of the festival is called 'Nit del Foc'. It is always the grandest night of fireworks and fires as it constitutes the grand finale.

There are several theories regarding the origins of the *Fallas* festival. Valencian carpenters used planks of wood to hang their candles on during the winter – these planks were called 'parots'. When Spring came, they no longer needed the wood, so it was burnt. Over time, the date of burning the 'parots' and the celebration of Saint Joseph coincided, so Saint Joseph was declared the patron saint of carpenters.

This tradition continued to change. The 'parot' was given clothes, so it looked like a person. Features of well known people in the town or villages were then added and today cardboard or soft cork is used to create *fallas* in excess of 30 metres!

Teaching activities

◆ Design your own *fallas* model. Write a list of materials that you would need to make it.

◆ Use the Internet to find out as much information about the festival. List the key facts.

◆ Design a poster listing the events for one of the days/ nights of the festival.

◆ Design a poster for the *fallas* competition.

◆ Write a diary entry giving information about the wake up call and so on.

◆ Brainstorm local characters that would inspire a *fallas* in your area.

◆ Do the children know the names of key politicians?

◆ Teach key politicians/leaders in Spain.

◆ Sketch a *fallas* based on a local celebrity. Briefly describe why you have chosen them.

◆ Draw a flow diagram to show how it is believed the *fallas* tradition began. Add small illustrations.

◆ Link to PSCHE. What behaviour would be expected of people at a San José celebration?

Vocabulario

un carnaval	a carnival
un rey	a king
una reina	a queen
un baile de máscara	a masked ball
una máscara	a mask
una carroza	a float
un disfraz	a costume
un desfile	a parade
una invitación	an invitation
lugar	place
fecha	date
hora	time

Spanish Festivals and Traditions
© *Nicolette Hannam, Michelle Williams and Brilliant Publications*

Las Fallas de San José

Nombre: _____   Fecha: _____

I can explain about the *Las Fallas de San José*.

Draw a picture of a *fallas* model. Use a dictionary to label the parts of the body or the clothes your model is wearing, in Spanish.

Extension activity

Make a PowerPoint presentation showing some of the events which take place during the festival.

El Festival de Flamenco de Jerez

Jerez Flamenco Festival

Background information

Flamenco has Gypsy or Arabic roots. The origins of flamenco are themes of hardship, desperation and hope. Flamenco dancing became extremely popular in Spanish cafes in the 1870s. Women, usually in burgundy dresses, would dance.

The dance is performed with a lot of energy and emotion. Now dancers wear very distinctive costumes and beat a rhythm with their heels, clicking castanets or clapping. Flamenco dresses are long and close fitting, designed to highlight the beauty of a woman's figure. Skirts often have ruffles around the hem. Heeled dance shoes and shawls usually accompany the dress, as well as simple jewellery. Women may choose to wear flowers or ornate combs in their hair. Flamenco is an opportunity to dress to impress!

Jerez de la Frontera is well known for many reasons, including its world famous sherry and its famous horse fair (described in more detail later in this book). At the end of February each year the city also hosts the International Flamenco Festival, also know as the Jerez Festival.
The festival takes place in and around the magnificent Villamarta Theatre where flamenco dancers from Spain and around the world come to perform flamenco concerts. Top artists perform over a two week period, with exquisite displays of flamenco music and dancing. Flamenco courses are available for people who would like to learn this fine art. There are also presentations, talks and discussions to increase people's knowledge of flamenco.

Teaching activities

◆ Use the Internet to find out as much information as you can about flamenco dancing.

◆ Draw a picture of the flamenco costumes worn by the women or men. Teachers could use the Internet to put some examples on the Interactive Whiteboard.

◆ Use the Internet to watch some flamenco dancing and listen to some flamenco music.

◆ Have a go at some flamenco dancing, using castanets or clapping.

◆ Design a poster to advertise the horse fair.

◆ Write a newspaper report. You could make up an eye-catching headline. Perhaps someone from your local town could go on holiday to Spain and wow everyone at the flamenco concert!

◆ Can you write a limerick about a flamenco dancer?

◆ Produce a mind map of different dances from around the world and add their characteristics.

Vocabulario

el vestido	dress
bailar	to dance
las castañuelas	castanets
el jerez	sherry
llevar el ritmo con las palmas	to clap

Flamenco dancing

Nombre: Fecha:

I know some key facts about flamenco dancing.

Draw and label a flamenco costume.

Write three key facts about flamenco dancing.

Extension activity
Can you name any traditional dances from any other countries?

Spanish Festivals and Traditions
© Nicolette Hannam, Michelle Williams and Brilliant Publications

Semana Santa

Holy Week (Easter)

Background information

April is an important month for Spanish fiestas. Semana Santa, or Holy Week, is a very important time across Spain. Easter marks a very important event in the Christian calendar and many people attend church. In some cities, groups of people get together and carry huge wooden floats depicting scenes from The Bible, There are also many special processions in towns and cities.

Often in Spain, men parade slowly and solemnly down the road wearing pointed hoods (*capirotes*) while the women stand in silence and watch, dressed in black. The pointed hoods represent those that were shamed by the crucifixion of Jesus. There may be a drum beating slowly and persistently to add to the solemnity of the occasion.

Palm Sunday is called *Domingo de Ramos* in Spain. Local churches will organise parades to mark the arrival of Jesus in Jerusalem. Palm leaves, or olive branches, will be carried. Each parade includes people dressed in different coloured tunics, some wearing a mask to hide their identity. The floats depict stories from The Bible, in particular of the death and resurrection of Jesus with images of the Virgin Mary, Jesus and the other saints. Many burn incense. Some villages play music, some a drum beat, and some choose silence.

One of the largest Easter parades takes place in Seville. On Easter Sunday the mood turns to jubilation, and traditional Spanish food is eaten in celebration of the resurrection. Sweet cakes such as *huesos de santo* and *rosquillas* are eaten and triumphant music accompanies the final floats.

Teaching activities

◆ Make some Easter cards or posters (see words in *Vocabulario* box).

> **Words for Easter cards**
>
> | Felices Pascuas | Happy Easter |
> | Querido … | Dear… (boy) |
> | Querida… | Dear… (girl) |
> | Saludos | Love from |

◆ Design *Una caza del huevo de Pascua* - an Easter egg hunt game (see page 27).

◆ Make a treasure map. Write instructions in Spanish for how to find the eggs.

◆ Hold a 'Decorate an Egg' competition. (Use either hard boiled eggs or pictures of eggs).

◆ Children could use the guided sheet on page 28 to compare Easter traditions in Britain and Spain.

◆ Read the children The Easter Story and discuss its significance.

◆ Can the children explain why the mood of Semana Santa changes from solemnity to jubilation?

◆ The children could design some floats, representing different stories from The Bible.

Vocabulario

Miércoles de Ceniza	Ash Wednesday
Cuaresma	Lent
Martes de Carnaval	Shrove Tuesday
Felices Pascuas	Happy Easter
el huevo de Pascua	Easter egg
el conejo de Pascua	Easter bunny
un polluelo	a chick
un cordero	a lamb
una cesta	a basket
una iglesia	a church
una campana	a bell
una cruz	a cross
querido…	dear … (boy)
querida …	dear … (girl)
un beso	a kiss
¿Te gustaría jugar?	Would you like to play?
te toca	your turn
me toca	my turn
tú ganas	you win
yo gano	I win
comienzo	start
fin	finish
avanza X casillas	move forward X spaces
retrocede X casillas	move back X spaces

Spanish Festivals and Traditions
© Nicolette Hannam, Michelle Williams and Brilliant Publications

Design 'una caza del huevo de Pascua' - an Easter Egg Hunt game

Design an Easter Egg Hunt game and play with a friend. See if you can play speaking just in Spanish! These words and phrases will help you:

Would you like to play?	¿Te gustaría jugar?
Your turn.	Te toca.
My turn.	Me toca.
You win.	Tú ganas.
I win.	Yo gano.
Start.	Comienzo.
Finish.	Fin.
Throw the dice.	Tira el dado.
Move forward 3 spaces.	Avanza tres casillas.
Move back 3 spaces.	Retrocede tres casillas.

Semana Santa

Nombre: Fecha:

I learned about *La Pascua* and how *Semana Santa* is celebrated in Spain.

Compare and contrast Easter in Spain and the United Kingdom. Write two similarities and two differences.

How do you celebrate Easter?
If you don't celebrate Easter, write about a different festival.

Extension activity
Use the Internet to find out some more information about how Easter is celebrated in different countries.

Spanish Festivals and Traditions
© Nicolette Hannam, Michelle Williams and Brilliant Publications

La Feria de abril

Seville's April Fair

Background information

Seville's April Fair, *La Feria de abril*, is a week-long festival of flamenco dancing, singing, eating and drinking. This festival began as a cattle market in 1847 and tents were put up to sell the animals. Today there are as many as one thousand tents or *casetas* for the one million people who come to the festival. Every year, a temporary gateway called *la portada* is erected. The tents are set up on the site of a permanent fairground and each street is named after a famous bullfighter. The fair is a place to enjoy friendships, with some sherry and tapas.

The festival officially begins on Monday at midnight, normally 2 weeks after *Semana Santa* (Holy Week). It opens with *el alumbrado* (the lighting) which is when half a million little lanterns are lit at once, particularly around the main gate.

At noon every day there is a procession called the *Paseo de Caballos*, local girls in their flamenco outfits are pulled through the city in beautiful carriages drawn by horses. A famous form of flamenco dance called *la sevillana* is performed. La s*evillana* is a type of folk music that originated in Seville. The accompanying four part dance followed later.

Many local people choose to dress in traditional costume. The men wear *traje corto* which is a suit with fitted trousers and a short jacket. Many men also wear wide-brimmed hats. Women dress brightly in *traje de gitano* which is gypsy style dresses, or flamenco dresses.

In the evening some of the year's top bullfights take place at the Plaza de Toros de Maestranza. Bull fighters are known as *matadores*. They dress in coloured suits, sometimes gold. They would never wear yellow as it is considered to be unlucky. A white shirt is worn with the suit. Also worn is a thin black tie, a coloured sash, knee high stockings, black shoes and a two cornered hat. A crucial part of the outfit is a pig's tail which is clipped to the back of the matador's head as he enters the ring, and cut once he retires from the ring. A matador's cape is only worn for the parade. It is hung on the fence at the side of the ring, in front of a friend, during the bull fighting. If the bullfighter has fought well he is taken out through *la puerta grande,* the main door, on the other men's shoulders.

People usually take food to eat whilst watching. Typical foods include; *tortilla de patatas, croquetas,* and lots of meats such as *jamón serrano* and *lomo de cerdo*.

The festival ends with a fireworks display the following Sunday, again at midnight.

Teaching activities

◆ List the activities which take place during, *La Feria de abril.*

◆ Plan a party for this fiesta.

◆ Design a poster advertising the event.

◆ Write a diary entry for a flamenco dancer in one of the carriages, or for a bullfighter.

◆ Research the traditional costumes. Draw and label them.

◆ Draw a matador, dressed ready to fight. What qualities would he need? Write these around the picture.

◆ Write a newspaper article about the event.

◆ Draw and label some of the food and drink available at the festival.

Vocabulario

casetas	tents
la portada	gateway
el alumbrado	the lighting
la sevillana	a form of flamenco
matador(a)	matador

La Feria de abril

Nombre: Fecha:

I learned about *La Feria de abril*.

Imagine you are celebrating with your friends …
What are you wearing?
What are you eating?
What are you drinking?
Draw and label your ideas.

Extension activity

Design a poster for tourists who may be visiting.

Las Cruces de mayo
May Crosses

Background information

The May Crosses Festival (Las *Cruces de mayo*) is celebrated in many parts of the world, especially in Latin America and Spain. In Spain, the festival holds special importance, especially in Córdoba, Andalucía which has the most famous celebration. Córdoba is the 10th largest city in Spain but is very popular as it has the feel of a small town, due to a historical centre and lots of history. It has a beautiful mosque, *la mezquita de Córdoba,* dating back to 785. It also has a synagogue, and some beautiful gardens with historical links to Christopher Columbus.

Saint Helen had a son who was in battle. Her son had a dream about a cross which was going to help him win his fight. Legend has it that a cross was then built and taken into battle – the war was then won. This inspired Saint Helen to go to Jerusalem in search of the cross Jesus was crucified on. Three crosses were found, but only one produced miracles, such as healing the sick. She then campaigned for people to continue to worship the cross, even after her death.

The May Crosses festival in Córdoba is more than just a festival, it is also a contest. People began decorating the crosses with flowers in 1953 and it has been a tradition ever since. There is also a parade called 'Battle of the Flowers', followed by a long procession of floats decorated with flowers. This celebration is to welcome springtime. Dancing, food, drink and fireworks are also an intrinsic part of this festival. Temporary bars are set up and there is drinking and dancing late into the night.

Teaching activities

◆ Use the photocopiable sheet on page 33 to draw and label a May Cross.

◆ Can you explain the story of the May Crosses?

◆ Can you find Córdoba on a map of Spain? How could we travel there?

◆ Why would people want to celebrate the arrival of Spring? Think of three reasons.

Vocabulario

las flores	flowers
las carrozas	floats
la primavera	spring
Las Cruces de mayo	May Crosses
el desfile	parade

Las Cruces de mayo

Nombre: Fecha:

I understand how and why *Las Cruces de mayo* is celebrated in Spain.

When are the *Cruces de mayo* in Spain?

How do the Spanish people celebrate?

Draw a picture of a May Cross below.

Extension activity

Use the Internet to find out the history of May Crosses.

La Feria del Caballo

Jerez Horse Fair

Background information

The Jerez Horse Fair is an exciting and lively event that takes place in May. The city of Jerez de la Frontera is famous for its sherry production and for its thoroughbred white Andalusian horses. The fair is one of the oldest in Spain. It began as a livestock show in 1284 but now it has grown into *una romería,* a magnet for horse lovers and equestrian enthusiasts from around the world. People bring their horses and have typical Spanish food. *La Feria de abril* is also *una romería.*

The fair takes place on the Gonzalo Hontoria Fair Ground in Jerez. On the first official day of the Fair, there is a spectacular firework display which marks the start of the festival which lasts 7 days. The event brings horsemen and women from around the world and events include stunning parades. The horsemen wear broad-brimmed hats, tight black trousers and short jackets, and the ladies wear flamenco dresses. The stallions are carefully manicured and dressed.

The Fair is a massive tourist attraction, attracting visitors from all over the world. Other events include exhibitions as well as music, dancing, eating and drinking. Children and adults can enjoy the large funfair. There are also bullfighting and flamenco displays. Visitors are encouraged to try many varieties of *jerez* which is similar to sherry and produced locally. There is also lots of wine on offer.

Teaching Activities

◆ Jerez is the home of several famous festivals – using a map, find out where Jerez is. Plot it on your own map of Spain.

◆ What is Jerez famous for?

◆ Find out some key facts about Jerez.

◆ How could you travel to Jerez?

◆ Design a poster for the Jerez Horse Fair.

◆ Write a diary entry for an imaginary visit to Jerez.

La Feria del Caballo

Nombre: Fecha:

I know about the Jerez Horse Fair.

Imagine you are at the horse fair. Describe what you can see and hear.

Draw and label a horse and its rider. What clothes are they wearing?

Extension activity

Horse-riding is a popular hobby. Draw and label your favourite hobby.

El día de la Madre
Mother's Day

Background information

In Spain, Mother's Day takes place on the first Sunday in May. It is celebrated in the same way as we celebrate it, giving cards and presents. Some children in Spain like to handcraft cards and gifts for their mothers. Usually everyone gathers for a family meal and ensures that mum is the centre of attention! In traditional Spanish families hierarchy is extremely important.

So in Spain, Mother's Day is in May, not March!

Teaching Activities

◆ Make a Mother's Day card (see words in *Vocabulario* box).

◆ Use the following words to draw and describe your mum.

> Mi madre es …
>
> | | |
> |---|---|
> | nice | simpática |
> | kind | amable |
> | beautiful | bonita / guapa |
> | clever | inteligente |
> | patient | paciente |

◆ Use the photocopiable sheet on p37 to describe an ideal Mother's Day.

◆ Design a medal or award for your mum.

◆ Write an acrostic poem using *Madre*.

◆ Make a list of celebrity mums. Do you know any famous Spanish celebrity mums?

◆ Revise family members in Spanish.

◆ Draw a family tree for your favourite character, for example, Bart Simpson.

Vocabulario

El día de la Madre	Mother's Day
Querida Mamá	Dear Mum
Te quiero	I love you
Querida	dear (girl)
Con amor	with love
Feliz día de la Madre	Happy Mother's Day
Mi madre es …	My mother is …
simpática	nice
amable	kind
bonita/guapa	beautiful
inteligente	clever
paciente	patient

El día de la Madre

Nombre: Fecha:

I understand how Mother's Day is celebrated in Spain.

When is Mother's Day celebrated in Spain?

How do we celebrate Mother's Day in the United Kingdom?

Describe an ideal Mother's Day below. Where could you go? What could you do? How could you make your mum feel extra special?

Extension activity

Can you make up a Mother's Day rhyme or poem in Spanish?

Las Hogueras de San Juan

Bonfires of Saint John

Background information

San Juan takes place from the 20th June till the 24th June (St John's Day, *El día de San Juan*) and is a huge party with bonfires, fireworks, music and dancing.

This festival marks the arrival of the summer solstice and is celebrated during the shortest night of the year. The celebrations of San Juan are of pagan origin and the basic characteristics of the festival are fire, water and the sun. Legend has it that the bonfires that burn on this night can cure various ailments by cleansing the body and the soul. It is even said that a bad year can be turned into a good one by simply jumping over the bonfires 3 times or more.

The party lasts for 3 to 4 days, with music, dancing, food and drink. *Pomada*, a drink made of gin and lemonade, is drunk and people throw handfuls of hazelnuts at each other – this is meant to be a sign of love!

As well as the bonfires that burn continuously, there are also *muñecos* or dolls that are burnt. This is usually done around midnight. Quite often the dolls are made up to represent local or national famous people and the burning of these dolls is supposed to bring good luck.

In the United Kingdom it is a time associated with magic, fairies and witches. Bonfires are also lit, traditionally in an attempt to strengthen the Sun. Many people travel to Stonehenge in Dorset, a ring of huge stones dating back almost 5000 years. On Midsummer Day, at sunrise, the sun shines directly in the middle of the circle of stones.

Teaching Activities

◆ Can you explain the story of the bonfires of San Juan?

◆ Design a *muñecos* doll based on a famous person.

◆ Do you know of any other actions that are meant to bring good luck?

◆ Design a Spanish invite to a bonfire party. Use the vocabulary on page 14 to help you.

◆ What type of food and drink would be available at an English bonfire party? How does it compare to Spanish food?

◆ Research San Juan on the Internet.

◆ Plan your own party with a sunshine theme. Think of costumes, invites, food, and so on.

Las Hogueras de San Juan

Nombre: Fecha:

I learned about the bonfires of San Juan.

Draw and label a picture of the bonfires of San Juan.

How is the summer soltice celebrated in different countries?

Extension activity

Imagine you are at a San Juan bonfire celebration. Write a postcard to a friend describing how you celebrated. Include what you did, and what you ate and drank.

Feliz Cumpleaños
Happy Birthday

Background information

In Spain, when it is your birthday, all your family gathers to wish you a Happy Birthday, which in Spanish is *¡Cumpleaños Feliz!*

Then, you eat a very big cake. On the cake, you have candles according to your age. Then, all the family sings *Cumpleaños Feliz* – 'Happy Birthday to you!' They use the same tune as we do.

After eating the cake, your family gives you presents and cards.

Spanish surnames

In Spain, everyone has two surnames. The first is that of your father's first surname and the second is your mother's first surname. It is always your father's surname that is carried forward to the next generation. For example:

Father's name: Juan Martín Pérez
Mother's name: María López García

Any children they might have will have the surnames Martín López

Common Spanish surnames are: García, Rodríguez, Martínez, Martín, Fernández, López, Sánchez and Pérez.

Some popular Spanish names and nicknames

Boys' names	Nickname	Girls' names	Nickname
Francisco	Paco/Fran	Pilar	Pili
José	Pepe	Juana	Pancha
Eduardo	Tito	Mercedes	Merche
Luis	Lucho	María Dolores	Lola
Antonio	Toni	Francisca	Paqui
Manuel	Manolo	Isabel	Isa
Jaime		María	
Ignacio		Ana	
Carlos		Laura	
		Leticia	

Spanish Festivals and Traditions
© *Nicolette Hannam, Michelle Williams and Brilliant Publications*

Saints days

In Spain, in common with many other predominantly Roman Catholic countries, people have Saint's Days as well as birthdays. There is a different Saint's Day for every day of the year, so traditionally you celebrate the day whose saint's name you share as well as your birthday. This is called *el día de tu santo*.

You would not sing a song or have a cake on your Saint's day, but you may get some presents and be congratulated with the greeting *¡Feliz Santo!*

Some days have more than one saint associated with it. The list below shows some of the Saint's Days for June (*junio*).

1	2	3	4	5	6	7
Alta Graciano Laura Candelaria Gracia Jimena Iñigo	Erasmo Marcelino Blandina Edelmira Ausonia	Olivia Kevin Cecilio Davino Clotilde Luciniano	Emma Querino Ruth Saturnina Noemí Rut	Eloísa Marcia Ígor Valeria Niconor Doroteo Bonifacio	Norberto Artemio Amancio Cándida Ismael	Roberto
8	**9**	**10**	**11**	**12**	**13**	**14**
Giraldo	Blanca Primo Feliciano Diana Efraín	Amalia Amelia Getulio Críspulo Asterio Trinidad Máximo	Benito Bernabé Aléida	Nazario Olimpo Cirilo	Antonio de Padua Antonia Joel Andoni	Félix Eliseo Digna
15	**16**	**17**	**18**	**19**	**20**	**21**
Lidia Vito Landelino Libia Benilde Eutrópia Crescencia	Ciro Aquilino Aureliano Siro Alina Regina Regis	Ismael Isauro Montano	Justo Marceliano Marina	Aurora	Elia Silverio Macario	Luis Demetria Terencio Raúl Gina Koldo Rodolfo
22	**23**	**24**	**25**	**26**	**27**	**28**
Albano Paulino	Alicia Apolo Inmaculada Walter Agripina	Juan Juana Ivana Joan Jon Iván Jean	Salomón Guillermo	Virgilio Pelayo Antelmo Alicia	Socorro Zoilo Ladislao Anecto Sansón	Marcela
29	**30**					
Ciro David Siro Paola Pablo Pedro	Marcial Leonila					

Documento nacional de identidad

Everybody over the age of 14 in Spain must have a National Identity Card, issued by the police. On the front it has a colour photograph and gives their name, and their two surnames. It would also include the holder's signature, an ID number, and issue date and an expiry date. The back has the holder's date of birth, both their parents' names, and their current address. ID cards are very important in Spain and one is needed to open a bank account, gain insurance and so on.

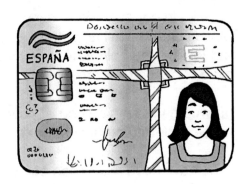

Teaching activities

◆ Make a birthday card or party invitation.

◆ Design your own ID card (documento nacional de identidad), with the following information on it:

Nombre:	Name
Cumpleaños:	Birthday
Edad:	Age
Vivo:	Where you live
Hermanos:	Brothers and sisters
El pelo:	Hair
Color de ojos:	Eye colour
Altura:	Height
Pasatiempos:	Hobbies

◆ Sing 'Cumpleaños Feliz' – to the tune of 'Happy Birthday to You':

> Cumpleaños Feliz,
> Cumpleaños Feliz,
> Te deseamos todos
> ¡Cumpleaños Feliz!

◆ Use the Internet to find out more about Saint's days. Practise saying Feliz santo (Happy Saint's Day!) to each other.

◆ Do a birthday survey using the Spanish months to find out when people in your class have their birthday.

¿Cuál es la fecha de tu cumpleaños?
Mi cumpleaños es el …

Nombre	Cumpleaños
Señora Williams	20 junio
Laura	17 abril

◆ Children could use the guided sheet on page 43 to compare traditional birthday celebrations in Spain and Britain.

Vocabulario

documento nacional de identidad	ID card
nombre	name
cumpleaños	birthday
edad	age
vivo	I live
hermanos	siblings
el pelo	hair
color de ojos	eyes
altura	height
pasatiempos	hobbies
Cumpleaños Feliz	Happy Birthday
Feliz Santo	Happy Saint's Day
un sondeo	a survey
¿Cuál es la fecha de tu cumpleaños?	When is your birthday?
¡Mi cumpleaños, es el …!	My birthday is …

Feliz Cumpleaños

Nombre: _____   Fecha: _____

I understand how birthdays are celebrated in Spain.

> If you were in Spain and it was your birthday, how would you celebrate?

> How did you celebrate your last birthday?

> Draw some presents you would like to receive and use a Spanish dictionary to help you label them.

Extension activity

Why do you have two 'birthdays' in Spain?

Las Fiestas de San Fermín

Running of the Bulls

Background information

From the 6th July to the 14th there is a week
long festival in honour of San Fermín, the
patron saint of Pamplona. Pamplona is in
Navarra in the Spanish Pyrenees. This is, once
again, a time for carnival with processions,
singing, dancing and delicious food and drink.
A special feature of this fiesta are *gigantes* or
giants. The giants are hollow, and carried on
the shoulders of people inside. The upper half
depicts a famous person, and the bottom half
is a skirt to disguise the carrier. The giants
often parade in pairs.

A *chupinazo* or rocket from the Town Hall
opens the celebrations at noon on the 6th
July. People shout *¡Viva San Fermín!* and the
singing, dancing and celebrating begins.

The next day, the 7th July, a figure of the saint
is carried through the streets as part of a
procession.

It is also tradition for characters in costumes with giant papier-mâché heads to take part in the
processions through the streets. These characters are called, *cabezudos*, *kilikis* and *zaldikos*.
Some of the characters pretend to chase the children, which is always very funny.

As with other carnivals, there are fireworks, music, dancing and great food and wine. However,
what makes this carnival stand out is the famous attraction of the *encierro*, or the daily 'bull-run'.
Each morning bulls are released to run about 800 metres through the streets to the bullring. This
only takes three minutes but, during this time, men try to run with the bulls through the narrow
streets. This can be very dangerous, but there are some strict rules in place! Runners must be 18
or over and must be in suitable attire. It is tradition to dress in white shirt, white trousers with a
red beret, red sash and red scarf.

In the evening bull fights are held. The bulls are not harmed, the bullfighter must get close
enough to place a metal ring over the bull's horn. Many Spanish people believe that if you
survive a close and scary encounter with a bull then you must have been protected by San
Fermín's cloak. Once again, there is a great party atmosphere and after the bull fights, the streets
are lined with people.

The *Fiestas de San Fermín* end on the 14th July with another procession, including the giants and
Pamplona's town band called, *la Pamplonesa*. Crowds gather at midnight, people carry candles
and meet in the town square where there are fireworks to mark the end of the Fiesta.

A Traditional 'San Fermín' Ryhme.

uno de enero	First of January
dos de febrero	Second of February
tres de marzo	Third of March
cuatro de abril	Fourth of April
cinco de mayo	Fifth of May
seis de junio	Sixth of June
Y siete de julio, San Fermín.	And on the seventh of July, it's 'San Fermín'.

Vocabulario

los gigantes	giants
el chupinazo	rocket
los cabezudos, kilikis, zaldikos	characters in processions
el encierro	Bull run
los fuegos	fireworks
el toro	bull
el disfraz	costume

Teaching activities

◆ Design and label a costume for the Fiesta.

◆ Design a giant for the Fiesta. Find some pictures of the *gigantes* to use as examples.

◆ Write a diary for the week of events during the Fiesta.

◆ Design a Fiesta picnic menu, using a dictionary.

◆ Write a newspaper report of the bull run.

◆ Draw and label a traditional bull runner.

◆ Make a list of people who *gigantes* may be based on in the UK.

◆ Make a poster of the bull-running rules.

◆ Research *la Pamplonesa* band. Draw and label the instruments they use.

Las Fiestas de San Fermín

Nombre: Fecha:

I understand how and why *Las Fiestas de San Fermín*, in Pamplona, is celebrated.

Imagine you are at the Fiesta. What can you see? What can you hear?

What happens during the *encierro*? What would you wear? Draw a picture of your outfit and label it.

Extension activity

Can you design one of the 'giants'. Use someone you know, a famous person, or even a teacher! Draw a picture on the back of this sheet. Include as much detail as you can.

Spanish Festivals and Traditions
© Nicolette Hannam, Michelle Williams and Brilliant Publications

Symbols of Spain

The Spanish flag

The Spanish national flag has three horizontal bands in red, yellow and then red and the royal coat of arms which is framed by the Pillars of Hercules guarding the entrance to the Mediterranean. The coat of arms is on the yellow stripe. Legend has it that the yellow represents the sand of the bull-fighting ring and the red is for the bull's blood.

Spanish Royal Family

Spain has a royal family. The King is called Juan Carlos I and his wife is Queen Sofía. Juan Carlos has been the King since 1975, his official title is *Su Majestad el Rey Don Juan Carlos*. The image of King Juan Carlos is on one side of the Spanish Euro.

The National Anthem

The Spanish National Anthem is called *La Marcha Real,* The Royal March. It is unusual because it has no official lyrics. The melody dates back to 1761, and was used as a march. Lyrics have been written for it and used, but none have been made official. New lyrics were suggested in 2008 but withdrawn after criticism. Below is one version that has been sung but remains unofficial:

Lyrics by Eduardo Marquina (1879-1946)

English language translation

Gloria, gloria, corona de la Patria,
soberana luz
que es oro en tu Pendón.
Vida, vida, futuro de la Patria,
que en tus ojos es
abierto corazón.
Púrpura y oro: bandera inmortal;
en tus colores, juntas, carne y alma están.
Púrpura y oro: querer y lograr;
Tú eres, bandera, el signo del humano afán.
Gloria, gloria, corona de la Patria,
soberana luz
que es oro en tu Pendón.
Púrpura y oro: bandera inmortal;
en tus colores, juntas, carne y alma están.

Glory, glory, crown of the Fatherland
sovereign light
which in your standard is gold
Life, life, future of the Fatherland,
in your eyes it is
an open heart
Purple and gold: immortal flag;
in your colours, together, flesh and soul are.
Purple and gold: to want and to achieve;
You are, flag, the sign of human effort.
Glory, glory, crown of the Fatherland
sovereign light
which in your standard is gold.
Purple and gold: immortal flag;
in your colors, together, flesh and soul are.

Patron saint

Saint James is the patron saint of Spain. He is known in Spain as *Santiago de Compostela*. He was a fisherman and one of Jesus' twelve disciples. Some people make a pilgrimage across northern Spain to the shrine of Saint James. James' emblem was the scallop shell. As a pilgrim Saint James carried a scallop shell and asked for it to be filled with enough food for one scoop. This included oats and barley, or perhaps beer and wine. On 25th July Saint James' festival is celebrated across Spain. Many people gather in streets and plazas and appeal for peace. This is followed by fireworks in honour of their patron saint.

The Pomegranate

The pomegranate is the symbol of the Spanish city of Granada. It can also be seen on the Spanish coat of arms. The word for pomegranate in Spanish is actually *granada* and many people believe the city was thus named because pomegranates grow here.

Bullfighting

The bull is another important symbol of Spain. Bullfighting is a traditional Spanish pastime and from March to October people go to special arenas to watch *la corrida de toros,* a bull fight. Many of the festivals in Spain centre around bulls and the bullfight itself is called *Fiesta Nacional.* The earliest record of a Spanish bull-fight is 1133, in celebration of the crowning of King Alfonso VIII. There are many bullfighting rings in Spain, the oldest ring is in the town of Ronda in Southern Spain. This famous tourist attraction was opened in 1785. The biggest bullfighting ring is in Madrid.

Pedro Romero from Ronda is the most famous Spanish bullfighter. He was born in 1754 and, during his career, was said to have killed over 5600 bulls. He was painted by the famous artist Francisco Goya. In traditional bullfighting there are three *toreros,* or *matadores,* each fight two bulls. The bulls are at least four years old and weigh 460–600 kg. Each matador has six assistants, two *picadores* (lancers) mounted on horseback, three *banderilleros* (flagmen), and a *mozo de espada* (sword page). Collectively they comprise a *cuadrilla* (entourage). The fierceness of the bulls is tested by the matador with his cape.

Flamenco

Flamenco came from Andalucía, influenced heavily by the local gypsy population, the *gitanos*. A great deal of the flamenco music and dance movements come from the Jewish tradition, as well as from Moorish culture. Three things make up flamenco, *el toque,* the guitar playing, *el cante*, the song, and *el baile*, flamenco dancing. Flamenco dancing appears to have its origins in the latter half of the eighteenth century.

Originally the dancing was set to no music, only singing and the clapping of hands. Some contemporary flamenco dancing still follows this tradition, though the use of the guitar and other instruments has been introduced. Flamenco dancing is an emotive dance style, the dancer expresses his or her emotions through the dance. During the dance, the dancer may clap their hands, kick their feet, click castanets, or jerk their body abruptly to demonstrate the desired emotion.

Other types of famous Spanish music and dance are the *fandango, pase doble, salsa* and *tango*.

Un abanico

Un abanico is a hand-held fan which can be seen in souvenir shops all over Spain. It is thought to have been used by Spanish nobility as early as the 14th Century and was made from palm leaves, silk and feathers.

Spanish Festivals and Traditions
© *Nicolette Hannam, Michelle Williams and Brilliant Publications*

The mantilla

The *mantilla* is the traditional head dress worn by women on special occasions, for example at a traditional Spanish wedding. They are usually made of lace or silk and worn over the head and the shoulders. Often a comb holds them in place. In Spain these special combs are known as *peineta*.

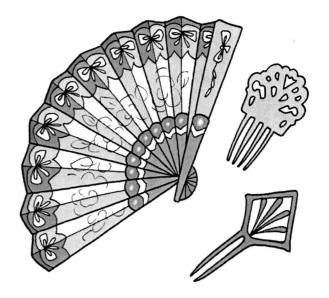

Las castañuelas

Las castañuelas are castanets, a traditional Spanish musical instrument. Castanets are a percussion instrument consisting of two concave shells joined together by string along the top edge. They are held in the hand and clicked together rhythmically. They are traditionally made of hardwood but, more recently, of fibre glass as they will last longer. Professional castanets players will have two pairs of castanets that each makes a different sound. They will hold a smaller pair in their right hand that will make a higher sound. In their left hand they will hold a larger pair that will make a lower sound. Castenets are most famous for accompanying flamenco dancing.

El Cid

Rodrigo Díaz de Vivar was a Spanish nobleman born around 1040. His nickname was *El Cid*, meaning 'the Chief'. He was a great leader in the King's army helping to defeat the Moors. *El Cid's* horse, *Babieca,* is one of the most famous horses in history. Legend has it that *El Cid* died just before a famous battle. His wife strapped his body, dressed in armour, to his horse to make the soldiers believe that their leader was still alive and they won this battle! The sword of *El Cid* can be seen in the Army Museum in Madrid and the tomb of *El Cid* and his wife *Jimena* can be found inside Burgos Cathedral.

Teaching activities

◆ Each child could colour the Spanish flag onto a sheet of paper. These could be stapled together onto string across the classroom to make a banner.

◆ Learn about flags around the world. Draw and colour some.

◆ Listen to the Spanish national anthem. Draw and colour the image that *La Marcha Real* creates in your mind.

◆ Examine the lyrics in both Spanish and English for one version of the national anthem. Do you like it? Does it represent the country of Spain? Would you change any of it?

◆ Discuss symbols in the United Kingdom (see box).

◆ Ask the children if they know any symbols for local sports teams. They could design one for a school team.

◆ Children could be introduced to Makaton, that uses symbols as a method of communication for disabled people.

Vocabulario

la corrida de toros	the bullfight
picadores	lancers
banderilleros	flagmen
mozo de espada	sword page
cuadrilla	entourage
el toque	guitar playing
el cante	the song
el baile	flamenco dancing
un abanico	hand held fan
mantilla	traditional head dress
peineta	hair comb
las castañuelas	castanets

Symbols of the United Kingdom

The Union flag, and each country's flag within it (see below)

England
Symbols: the three lions, red rose (appears on the England Rugby Team kit), oak tree
Patron saint: St George (23rd April)
Flag: the red cross (cross of St George)

Scotland
Symbols: the thistle, bagpipes, tartan kilts
Patron saint: St Andrew (30th November)
Flag: white diagonal cross (called a saltire) on a blue background (cross of St Andrew)

Northern Ireland
Symbols: shamrock, harp, Celtic cross
Patron saint: St Patrick (17th March)
Flag: red diagonal cross (saltire) on a white background (cross of St Patrick)

Wales
Symbols: leeks, daffodils, red dragon.
Patron saint: St David (1st March)
Flag: red dragon on a white (top) and green (bottom) background

You could also discuss The Royal Family.

Spanish symbols

Nombre: Fecha:

I can recognize some Spanish symbols.

Look carefully at this picture of the Spanish coat of arms. Sketch and colour it in the next box.

Now design a coat of arms for Britain. Write a brief description of it as well.

Extension activity

Design a coat of arms for your school or your family.

Cuentos de hadas

Fairy stories

Background information

In Spain, children read and learn fairy stories, just like children all over the world.

Here are some titles of fairy tales in Spanish:

Caperucita Roja	Little Red Riding Hood
Cenicienta	Cinderella
Blancanieves	Snow White
La Historia de Los Tres Cerditos	The Three Little Pigs

Teaching activities

◆ Read a simple fairy tale for the children to act out. Familiarize them with the key vocabulary first. Display the fairy tale for the children to follow as you read it aloud.

◆ Ask the children to respond with physical gestures when they hear key words or character's names. Use lots of repetition.

◆ Use a simple Spanish fairy tale in a sequencing activity. Jumble up key sentences for the children to reorder.

◆ Ask the children to pretend to be a character, for example Red Riding Hood. What could we ask her? Children could ask them their name / age / favourite colour, and so on.

◆ Can the children use simple Spanish to change the beginning or the ending of the story? They could be given a choice of two endings, in Spanish, that they have to translate and choose.

◆ What story do you think these rhymes come from?

Espejito, espejito, di	Mirror, mirror on the wall
¿Quién es la más bella de todas las mujeres?	Who is the fairest of them all?
Tú eres, oh reina, la más hermosa de todas las mujeres.	You, oh Queen, are the fairest in the land

Vocabulario

Había una vez …	Once upon a time …
el rey	the king
la reina	the queen
la princesa	the princess
el príncipe	the prince
la bruja	the witch
el hada	the fairy
el hada madrina	fairy godmother
el bosque	the wood/the forest
el palacio	the palace
el lobo	the wolf
la abuela	grandma
los siete enanitos	the seven dwarfs
una varita mágica	a magic wand
la bestia	the beast
el monstruo	the monster
el leñador	the woodcutter
el palacio	the palace
una gran fiesta	a big party
sus hermanastras	her stepsisters
la madrastra	the stepmother
un zapato de vidrio	a glass slipper
los tres cerditos	the three little pigs
el gran y malvado lobo	the big, bad wolf
una casa de paja	a house made of straw
una casa de madera	a house made of sticks
una casa de ladrillos	a house made of bricks

¡No, no, por nada en el mundo te dejaré entrar!	No, no, I'll never let you in!
¡Entonces soplaré y soplaré y tu casa tiraré!	Then I'll huff and I'll puff 'til I blow your house down!

◆ Children could match Spanish characters names and key words to Spanish fairy tale titles. Suggested answers are in the chart below:

Caperucita Roja (Little Red Riding Hood)	Blancanieves (Snow White)	Cenicienta (Cinderella)	Los Tres Cerditos (The Three Little Pigs)
Caperucita Roja (Little Red Riding Hood) Había una vez ... (once upon a time ...) el bosque (the wood) el lobo (the wolf) mi abuela (my Grandma) el leñador (the woodcutter)	Blancanieves (Snow White) Había una vez ... (once upon a time ...) el rey (the king) la madrastra (the stepmother) el palacio (the palace) el príncipe (the prince) los siete enanitos (the seven dwarves) el bosque (the wood)	Cenicienta (Cinderella) sus hermanastras (her stepsisters) la madrastra (the stepmother) el rey (the king) el príncipe (the prince) el hada madrina (the Fairy Godmother) un zapato (a shoe/slipper) una gran fiesta (a big party) el palacio (the palace)	Los Tres Cerditos (The Three Little Pigs) Había una vez ... (once upon a time ...) el gran y malvado lobo (the big, bad wolf) una casa de paja (a house made of straw) una casa de madera (a house made of sticks) una casa de ladrillos (a house made of bricks)

◆ Use the Red Riding Hood dialogue on page 55. Children could act it out in assembly. Or each phrase could be given to the children to match to a character. A translation is given below:

(Caperucita Roja meets the wolf in the forest.)	
Caperucita Roja: ¡Hola! Me llamo Caperucita Roja.	Hello. My name is Little Red Riding Hood.
El lobo: ¡Hola! ¿Dónde vas en este día?	Hello! Where are you going?
Caperucita Roja: Voy a llevar unos pasteles a mi abuela.	I'm taking these cakes to my granny.
(The wolf goes to Grandma's house, dressed as Caperucita Roja.)	
El lobo: ¡Hola! ¿Cómo estás?	Hello! How are you?
El abuela: Muy bien, ven adentro.	I'm well, come in.

(The wolf eats Grandma and disguises himself as her).

| El lobo: | ¿Hay alguién? | Is anybody there? |

Caperucita Roja: Soy yo, abuela, Caperucita Roja. ¿Puedo entrar? | It's me, grandma, Little Red Riding Hood. Can I come in?

| El lobo: | Ven adentro. | Come in. |

Caperucita Roja: ¡Abuela, qué ojos tan grandes tienes! | Oh Grandma, what big eyes you have!

| El lobo: | Para verte mejor, cariño. | All the better to see you with. |

Caperucita Roja: ¡Abuela, qué orejas tan grandes tienes! | Oh Grandma, what big ears you have!

| El lobo: | Para oírte mejor, cariño. | All the better to hear you with. |

Caperucita Roja: ¡Abuela, qué dientes tan grandes tienes! | Oh Grandma, what big teeth you have!

| El lobo: | ¡Para **comerte** mejor, cariño! | All the better to eat you with! |

| Caperucita Roja: ¡Socorro! | Help! |

(The woodcutter runs in the house and saves Caperucita Roja – and cuts open wolf's stomach to save Grandma.)

Caperucita Roja
& abuela: ¡Gracias! | Thank you!

El fin | *The end*

◆ Children could use the guided sheet on page 56 to make up their own picture story of a fairy tale.

Spanish Festivals and Traditions
© *Nicolette Hannam, Michelle Williams and Brilliant Publications*

Caperucita Roja

(Caperucita Roja meets the wolf in the forest.)

Caperucita Roja: ¡Hola! Me llamo Caperucita Roja.

El lobo: ¡Hola! ¿Dónde vas en este día?

Caperucita Roja: Voy a llevar unos pasteles a mi abuela.

(The wolf goes to Grandma's house, dressed as Caperucita Roja.)

El lobo: Hola, ¿Cómo estás?

El abuela: Muy bien, ven adentro.

(The wolf eats Grandma and disguises himself as her).

El lobo: ¿Hay alguien?

Caperucita Roja: Soy yo, abuela, Caperucita Roja. ¿Puedo entrar?

El lobo: Ven adentro.

Caperucita Roja: ¡Abuela, qué ojos tan grandes tienes!

El lobo: Para verte mejor, cariño.

Caperucita Roja: ¡Abuela, qué orejas tan grandes tienes!

El lobo: Para oírte mejor, cariño.

Caperucita Roja: ¡Abuela, qué dientes tan grandes tienes!

El lobo: Para **comerte** mejor, cariño.

Caperucita Roja: ¡Socorro!

(The woodcutter runs in the house and saves CR – and cuts open wolf's stomach to save Grandma.)

Caperucita Roja
& abuela: ¡Gracias!

El fin

Cuentos de hadas

Nombre: Fecha:

I have learnt about some fairy tales in Spanish.

Can you make up your own picture story of a fairy tale?

Can you draw and label some of your own Spanish fairy tale characters?

Spanish Festivals and Traditions
© Nicolette Hannam, Michelle Williams and Brilliant Publications

La Tomatina

The World's biggest food fight – an hour of tomato slinging

Background information

This is basically a huge tomato battle where more than 125,000 tons of over-ripe tomatoes are thrown in the streets. People attend from all over the world.

This is a festival held on the last Wednesday of August every year in the town of Buñol in the Valencia region of Spain.

The origin of this fiesta is unknown, but one of the most popular theories is that angry townspeople attacked the city councilmen with tomatoes during a town celebration in 1945. People enjoyed this so much that it has become a tradition with as many as 40,000 tourists flocking to this event.

The week long fiesta has music, dancing, parades and fireworks. On the night before the tomato fight people compete in a paella cooking contest. Paella is a very famous Spanish dish consisting of rice and meat, seafood or vegetables. It is made in a wide, shallow dish. Saffron is usually cooked with the rice to make the dish yellow in appearance.

La Tomatina begins at around 10am. Water cannons signal the start of the battle which lasts one hour. Water cannons are also fired to signal the end of the battle. Tomatoes must be squished a little beforehand, for safety reasons, and buildings and shops must be covered in huge plastic covers for protection.

Teaching activities

◆ Draw a picture of *La Tomatina*.

◆ Draw and label the ingredients for paella. You could label the ingredients in English, or use a dictionary to help you label them in Spanish.

◆ You could create some Maths word problems based on quantities using a *La Tomatina* theme.

◆ You could write a newspaper report of the event.

◆ You could act out a news report and interview someone who took part.

◆ You could write a persuasive letter to your headteacher persuading him / her to allow you to re-enact *La Tomatina* in your playground!

◆ You could write an acrostic poem using *La Tomatina*.

La Tomatina

Nombre: Fecha:

I know about the festival, *La Tomatina*.

Imagine that you are at *La Tomatina*. Draw a picture of what is happening. Include speech and thought bubbles from some of the characters.

Extension activity
Use the Internet to find out about the town of Buñol.

Spanish Festivals and Traditions
© Nicolette Hannam, Michelle Williams and Brilliant Publications

Planning a holiday

Background information

Spain is the second largest country in size in Europe, after France. It has the fifth largest population. Spain has more than 2200km of mainland coastline and is only 16km apart from Africa. Portugal lies on the western border of Spain. It also borders the Atlantic Ocean, the Mediterranean Sea, the Bay of Biscay, and France. France and Spain share the Pyrenees Mountains.

Spain also includes the four Balearic Islands of Mallorca, Menorca, Ibiza and Formentera and the seven Canary Islands, Cueta Melilla and several very small islands off the coast of Morocco.

Spain has 5 mountain ranges and is the highest country in Europe after Switzerland. Spain's highest mountain is called Teide and is in Tenerife in the Canary Islands. It is in fact a dormant volcano. The Sierra Nevada is a mountain range in southern Spain which has the highest point on the Spanish mainland.

The capital of Spain is Madrid which has a population of 5.42 million. The longest river is the *Tajo* which is 1007 metres long. It is known as the Tagus in English. It delivers a lot of the electric power in Spain through its large dams. It runs through Spain, into Portugal and into the Atlantic Ocean.

Spain has a huge tourist population – the highest in Europe. More than 50 million people visit Spain each year.

Some of the famous landmarks in Spain are the 'Sagrada Familia' in Barcelona, the Guggenheim Museum in Bilbao and the *Alhambra* in Granada. The 'Sagrada Familia' is a huge Roman Catholic Church, designed by Antoní Gaudí in Barcelona. Construction began in 1882 and the building is still being developed to this day. Plans hope that it will be finished in 2026 which will mark the 100th anniversary of Gaudí's death. The Guggenheim Museum is in Bilbao and on the banks of the Nervión River. It holds contemporary and modern art. The *Alhambra* is a palace in southern Spain. It has beautiful Islamic architecture and is extremely popular with tourists.

Spanish people are particularly proud of their artistic culture, in particular the artists Picasso, Miró and Dalí.

Some famous Spanish artists are:

Diego Velázquez	17th Century
Francisco Goya	18th Century
Joaquín Sorolla	19th Century
Pablo Picasso/Salvador Dalí/Joan Miró	20th Century

Pablo Picasso produced more works of art than any other artist, around 13,500 paintings and 100,000 engravings.

Houses

Some Spanish houses are painted white or a pale colour on the outside. Light colours reflect the sun and help keep the house cool, especially during the hot summer months. The floors are also tiled for the same reason. Windows usually have shutters or blinds too.

In Spain, the Spanish language is officially called Castilian, *el castellano*. Other Spanish languages are spoken there too, for example, Catalan, *el catalán*, Galician, *el gallego* and Basque, *el vasco*.

Travelling to Spain

We can travel to Spain by ferry, aeroplane or train. Flying to Spain is easy and quite affordable now. Popular British airports are London Heathrow, Gatwick, Stansted or Leeds Bradford. You can fly to almost every major city in Spain, depending on which airline you choose. You can also take the ferry to Spain, crossing from Plymouth or Portsmouth to Santander or Bilbao.

Where else is Spanish spoken?

Spanish is the official language of 23 countries and is spoken worldwide as a first language by 350 million people. Spanish is the third most widely spoken language after Chinese and English. Mexico, Cuba, Chile, Argentina, Columbia, Puerto Rico and Nicaragua are just some of the South American countries where Spanish is spoken.

Teaching Activities

◆ Look at a map of Spain and give the children some key facts about Spain. Make comparisons to the United Kingdom in your discussion. If you have an Interactive Whiteboard, you can find a map of Spain in the Gallery. If not, there are many good examples on the Internet. Discuss main towns, key geographical features and well-known landmarks.

◆ The children could plan a holiday to Spain, or another Spanish-speaking country, following your discussion.

◆ Children could pretend to be on holiday in Spain and write a postcard home.

◆ Children could plan their dream holiday to a destination of their choice. They need to think about the climate, which languages are spoken there and the activities available. (See guided sheet on page 62.)

◆ Children could write about the best holiday they have ever had and explain why.

◆ Use weather sites on the Internet to compare weather in a locality in Spain, eg in Bilboa in the north or Málaga in the south with that in your locality, over a period of time.

◆ The children could work in pairs to draw a Venn diagram, comparing Spain and the United Kingdom.

◆ Children could make a poster advertising either Britain or Spain as an excellent holiday destination. They should use a range of persuasive techniques (link to Literacy work).

◆ More able could highlight all the places on a world map where Spanish is spoken.

◆ Do a survey to find out what other languages are spoken in the school. Locate the country/ countries where these languages are spoken using maps, atlases and globes.

◆ Talk to children about which other languages they would like to learn and why.

Planning a holiday

Nombre: Fecha:

I can plan a trip.

Where are you travelling from?	Which mode(s) of transport will you use?

Which mode(s) of transport will you use?

train	❑	bus	❑
aeroplane	❑	boat/ferry	❑
car	❑	walk	❑
bike	❑	other	❑

Where are you travelling to?

Where will you stay? What type of accommodation?

What will you do on your trip? Draw and describe some activities.

Is your holiday to a popular tourist destination? Explain your answer.

Extension activity
Where else in the world would you like to travel? Explain why.

Spanish Festivals and Traditions
© Nicolette Hannam, Michelle Williams and Brilliant Publications

How is Spanish culture incorporated into our everyday life?

Background information

Due to the amount of travelling that now takes place across and around the world, the cultures of different countries can be transferred to new places more easily. Some people immigrate to different countries and take traditions with them. Others bring back ideas from travels and holidays.

Popular songs and films demonstrate different cultures and influence audiences. Television programmes show us places and recipes we have never seen before, and inspire us to try new things.

Large supermarkets are a great place to examine the influence of different cultures through the food that is sold. Spanish food and wine is popular in our supermarkets and tapas restaurants are now common in large towns and cities. Olive oil is a typical Spanish product, as are olives, oranges, wine, *jamón serrano* (a type of ham) and *chorizo* (garlic sausage).

In schools, children have the opportunity to learn about interesting and diverse religious festivals.

Teaching Activities

◆ Use the guided sheet on page 64 to look at similarities and differences between two countries, perhaps Spain and the United Kingdom. Develop into a discussion on cultural diversity.

◆ Discuss Spanish influences on life in the United Kingdom. Topics could include language, food, drink, sport, fashion and so on.

◆ Draw and label Spanish influences in the UK.

◆ Design a tapas menu. (See page 83.)

◆ Set a homework task for the children to visit a supermarket, find 3 Spanish items for sale, and record what they are.

◆ Discuss products from Spain. Why are they different to products from the UK? Discuss the different climates and hence the different goods produced.

Comparing cultures

Nombre: Fecha:

I can compare two countries.

Name	Flag
Population	
Size	
Languages spoken	
Famous landmarks	Major cities/towns
Famous food	Additional information

Name	Flag
Population	
Size	
Languages spoken	
Famous landmarks	Major cities/towns
Famous food	Additional information

Spanish Festivals and Traditions
© Nicolette Hannam, Michelle Williams and Brilliant Publications

La Fiesta de la Vendimia
Grape Harvest Festival

Background information

La Fiesta de la Vendimia is the Grape Harvest Festival. In Jerez, a fiesta is held every year on the weekend nearest the 8th September to celebrate the wine harvest. Jerez is in Andalucía, near the port of Cádiz and is famous for its sherry.

In winemaking, the year in which the grapes are made into wine is called its 'vintage' and for the fiesta there is a Queen of the Vintage who leads the procession. The Queen and her helpers are carried on huge floats decorated with grapes and vine leaves. They are dressed in white with blues scarves and they throw sweets to the children in the crowd. After the floats, men dressed in costumes and masks parade and then there are fireworks.

On the following Sunday, there is a mass to bless the grapes for the next season.

Teaching Activities

◆ What is *la Vendimia*?

◆ Design your own wine label using the name of your school, for example Vino Battyeford.

◆ Research the wine-making process and write some instructions.

◆ Make a postcard to send home from an imaginary trip to *La Vendimia*.

◆ Plan and write a discursive text: Should children be allowed to drink wine at home?

Vocabulario	
el vino	wine
el jerez	sherry
las uvas	grapes
las hojas de parra	vine leaves
la reina	Queen
las carrozas	floats
los caramelos	sweets
una botella	bottle
una etiqueta	label
una viña	vineyard

La Fiesta de la Vendimia

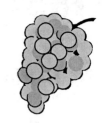

Nombre: Fecha:

I learned about the fiesta _La Vendimia_.

Harvest Festivals are held in countries all over the world.

Use the internet to find out about Harvest in two countries – write 2 lists.

Country 1: | **Country 2:**

Extension activities

◆ Write a letter to a Spanish person explaining about Harvest Festival in Britain.

Spanish Festivals and Traditions
© Nicolette Hannam, Michelle Williams and Brilliant Publications

La Vuelta ciclista a España

Annual cycle race

Background information

This is the annual cycle race around Spain held from the 4th – 26th September and is approximately 3,000km long. The race starts in León and finishes in Madrid. It first took place in 1935 with 50 competitors and is now the third largest cycle race in Europe. It now consists of 20 stages. Competitors are timed in each stage. The fastest rider has the honour of wearing the golden jersey for the following stage. Spanish people love to cheer on the competitors with banners, and many enjoy a picnic on the roadside. The other two famous European cycle races are the *Tour de France* and the *Giro d'Italia*.

Teaching Activities

◆ Find out which other countries hold cycle races.

◆ Use a map of Spain to trace the route which is taken.

◆ Use the Internet to find out about a famous Spanish cyclist.

◆ Which other sports do they play in Spain?

◆ Choose a famous Spanish sports person and write a profile about them.

◆ Which attributes does an excellent cyclist need? List and explain them.

◆ Make a small banner in Spanish to cheer the competitors on.

◆ Research similarities and differences between the *Tour de France* and *La Vuelta*.

Vocabulario

la vuelta ciclista	cycle race
la bici	bike
ganador/ora	winner
Maillot amarillo or Jersey de Oro	Golden jersey

A typical school day in Spain

Background information

Preschool education is split with two cycles of three years each. The first cycle, *la guardería infantil*, is for children up to 3 . The second cycle, la *escuela infantil*, is free and is for children aged 3 to 6.

Compulsory primary school, la *escuela primaria*, begins at 6 years old and lasts for six years. It is divided into three 2-year cycles.

Compulsory secondary school, la *escuela secundaria,* is for four years, from 12 to 16, and is divided into two 2-year cycles. It leads to the *Graduado en Educación Secundaria Obligatoria*. This certificate is required if you want to continue to higher secondary education.

Higher secondary is for two years, from age 16-18, at the end of which students study for *Título de Bachillerato* or *Título de Técnico*. Some 55% of students stay in school until they are 18.

The school year is from September to June. School hours vary from place to place, according to the type of school and even the time of year. Primary school hours are typically from 9am – 5pm, with a 2-hour break for lunch. Children can usually stay for school dinners and there are extra-curricular activities to occupy them during the long lunch break. In the hot summer months of June and September, school hours are shorter – 9am to 1pm – with no afternoon lessons.

Secondary schools generally start earlier (eg 8am) and finish about 2pm, with no afternoon lessons.

The organization of the academic system in Spain

Escuela primaria

Spain	UK	Age
Primero de Primaria	Year 2	6–7
Segundo de Primaria	Year 3	7–8
Tercero de Primaria	Year 4	8–9
Cuarto de Primaria	Year 5	9–10
Quinto de Primaria	Year 6	10–11
Sexto de Primaria	Year 7	11–12

Escuela secundaria

Spain	UK	Age
1º de la ESO*	Year 8	12–13
2º de la ESO*	Year 9	13–14
3º de la ESO*	Year10	14–15
4º de la ESO*	Year 11	15–16
1º de Bachillerato	Year 12	16–17
2º de Bachillerato	Year 13	17–18

*ESO = Educación Secundaria Obligatoria

Teaching Activities

◆ Visit a website and find out what Spanish children are eating for their lunch today. Compare to your own school menu.

◆ Children could draw or write their meal, and the Spanish meal to compare.

◆ Children could revise the names of the fruit and vegetables they have learnt as a link to healthy eating. They could draw and label them

◆ You could teach the names of some subjects in Spanish schools and children could design a timetable, taking into account the long lunch hour. They could then compare this to their own timetable.

◆ You could display your class timetable in Spanish and ask children which lessons they have had, or will have next.

◆ Design a brochure to welcome newcomers to your school and explain your routines.

◆ Children could copy the Spanish menu and decorate it, drawing a picture of each dish. The audience could be Spanish children. See the photocopiable sheet on page 70 for an example of a Spanish school menu that the children could decorate. Older children could carefully copy the Spanish onto a plain sheet and decorate.

◆ Children could list food they do and do not like, using a dictionary to help them write in Spanish.

Vocabulario

la guardería infantil	creche
el jardín de infancia	nursery
la escuela primaria	primary school
la escuela secundaria	secondary school
las matemáticas	maths
el inglés	English
la geografía	geography
el español	Spanish
el dibujo	art
la informática	ICT
la tecnología	DT

A typical Spanish lunch

Nombre: Fecha:

I can describe a typical Spanish school dinner

Menú

PRIMER PLATO:

Sopa de verduras

SEGUNDO PLATO:

Pollo

Patatas bravas

Ensalada verde

POSTRE:

Flan

Extension activities

What did you have for your dinner today?

Which dinner would you prefer? Why?

Spanish Festivals and Traditions
© Nicolette Hannam, Michelle Williams and Brilliant Publications

Comparing pastimes and everyday life

Background information
Spanish children have similar hobbies to British children. Perhaps, due to the increase in warmer weather, Spanish children may spend more time outdoors. Everyday life is also very similar. School days may differ slightly, and children do not wear uniform to school. The most beneficial way to compare everyday life is to show video clips of Spanish children to begin discussions. It will most likely continue into a discussion about stereotypes and their inaccuracies.

Teaching activities

◆ Children could compare their own pastimes/hobbies with Spanish children, using the guided sheet on page 72. They will find that they are very similar.

◆ Discuss similarities and differences in everyday life between Spain and the United Kingdom.

◆ Children could mime activities and say what they are doing in Spanish. Alternatively, you could play a game of *Simon dice* (Simon Says).

◆ Try this hot potato activity. Give each table a large sheet of paper. Each table has two minutes to write as much as they know about the lives of Spanish and English children. Pass the sheets around (giving two minutes for each sheet), until each table has written on every sheet. Share and discuss findings.

◆ Children could compile a list of questions they would like to ask a Spanish person.

◆ If possible, invite a native speaker in to talk about their hobbies as a child.

◆ Children could write a postcard home from Spain detailing the activities they have done, in Spanish.

Vocabulario

mis pasatiempos	my hobbies
juego al …	I play …
fútbol	football
rugby	rugby
tenis	tennis
hockey	hockey
golf	golf
toco …	I play
el piano	the piano
el violín	the violin
la guitarra	the guitar
voy en monopatín	I go skateboarding
monto en bici	I ride my bike
voy de compras	I go shopping
monto a caballo	I go horse riding
nado	I swim
bailo	I dance
escucho música	I listen to music
veo la tele	I watch TV
voy al cine	I go to the cinema
juego al ordenador	I play computer games

Comparing pastimes

Nombre: Fecha:

I can compare children's pastimes in Britain and Spain.

Look at the information about a child in Spain. Then complete the box, in the same style, with information about yourself.

Name	José	Self-portrait	
Date of birth	10 de enero		
Place of birth	Madrid		
Favourite food	Tortilla	**Hobbies**	música (music) baile (dance) cine (cinema) fútbol (football)
Favourite drink	Zumo de naranja		

Name		Self-portrait
Date of birth		
Place of birth		
Favourite food		**Hobbies**
Favourite drink		

Spanish Festivals and Traditions
© Nicolette Hannam, Michelle Williams and Brilliant Publications

El Día de la Hispanidad
Spanish National Day

Background information

Spain's national holiday is held on the 12th October. It is a day of parades presided over by the Spanish King. The day commemorates the date in 1492 when Christopher Columbus, or 'Cristóbal Colón', as he is known in Spain, discovered the Americas. Christopher was born in Genova in Italy in 1451 and died in 1506. His tomb is in Seville Cathedral and is held by statues of four kings. Each statue represents a kingdom of Spain – León, Castilla, Aragón and Navarra.

He decided from an early age that he wanted to be an explorer. Columbus had an idea that it was possible to sail westward from Europe to the Orient rather than taking the usual and longer eastern route to Asia. He wanted to profit from the spice trade here. Columbus needed people to sponsor his expedition, and eventually sought backing from King Ferdinand and Queen Isabella of Spain. He promised to find them new lands, spices, money and more people to become Christian. They also gave him three ships; the Nina, the Pinta and the Santa María. He completed four expeditions in total which were hailed as great successes. He returned to Spain to a hero's welcome and was given the titles of Admiral of the Seven Seas and Viceroy of the Indies.

Columbus took trade items on his expeditions so that he could bring back new things to Europe. He took items such as glass beads, brass rings, knitted caps, gold, silver, pearls and spices. He brought back many new items and ideas about different cultures. He was given fruits, flowers, feathers and birds as gifts. He traded his items for foreign goods such as plants, animals (including horses, cows, pigs and chickens), and a variety of goods including gold (in the form of crowns, masks, ornaments, nuggets and dust). He learnt new ways to cultivate crops and prepare food. In particular he brought back new crops including wheat, rice, coffee, bananas and olives. And so the trading began. Unfortunately Columbus is also reputed to have spread some European diseases from his sailors.

Teaching Activities

◆ Find out as much information as you can about Christopher Columbus.

◆ Write a profile of Christopher Columbus.

◆ Write a list of things Christopher brought back from his travels.

◆ Plot the route of Christopher Columbus on a map.

◆ Write to Christopher Columbus thanking him for his bravery and for the items that he brought back.

Vocabulario

las plantas	plants
los animales	animales
los caballos	horses
las vacas	cows
los cerdos	pigs
las gallinas	chickens
el oro	gold
la cosecha	crops
el trigo	wheat
el arroz	rice
el café	coffee
los plátanos	bananas
las aceitunas	olives

El Día de la Hispanidad

Nombre: Fecha:

I understand how and why *El Día de la Hispanidad* is celebrated in Spain.

Draw and label some of the things that Christopher Columbus brought back with him. Use a dictionary to help label the things in Spanish.

Extension activities

◆ Use a world map to highlight the places Christopher Columbus discovered.

Spanish Festivals and Traditions
© Nicolette Hannam, Michelle Williams and Brilliant Publications

Halloween

Halloween

Background information

Halloween began in The British Isles as a festival called Samhain. It was believed that on this day sprits rose from the dead, so people wore masks to scare bad spirits away. Centuries later, in the 1840s, Halloween found its way to America, with the Irish immigrants. Over time, it developed into the children's festival that we now know.

The Spanish began to hear about it from tourists, and in their English lessons. The Spanish believe that black cats are bad luck, particularly around Halloween time. They feel very nervous if a black cat crosses their path, enters their home, or comes aboard their ship!

Also in parts of Spain a traditional pastry – the Bones of the Holy, *Huesos de Santo* - is eaten at this time. It is shaped like skulls, contains anise seeds and is coated in an orange glaze.

In Spain the children now dress up in scary costumes for Halloween or el *Día de las Brujas* (Day of the Witches). People have parties or go out for a meal. Trick-or-treating is now more common. Children go from house to house and collect sweets. In some parts of Spain it is more common for children to trick-or-treat along the cafés and shops rather than houses. Shopkeepers and café owners have baskets of sweets ready for the children who are dressed up. Adults are encouraged to enjoy a coffee or a glass of Rioja while the children collect sweets. Pumpkins are also popular. People carve a scary face and put a candle inside.

In Spain, Halloween is a three-day celebration. Halloween is not only about honouring the dead, but also a celebration of the continuity of life. Older members of society still refer back to an older tradition of honouring the dead at the end of October and use the time to visit cemeteries, honouring saints and going to religious ceremonies. Symbolically, in Spain, Halloween is seen as a time to burn off bad luck with bonfires and clear dark energies. Some families spend the day after Halloween (1st November), All Saints Day, el *Día de Todos los Santos*, tidying family burial plots (see page 85).

Finally, on the 2nd November, families observe the customs and rituals of All Souls' Day, *el Día de los Muertos*.

Teaching Activities

◆ Use flashcards to teach the children Halloween-related vocabulary. Children could then use cards made from page 77 to play Pelmanism (Pairs) or Snap to reinforce the vocabulary.

◆ Children could write a Spanish Halloween word each and draw a picture to match it.

◆ Link to Literacy – children could write a spooky Halloween story.

◆ Anagrams – you could muddle up the letters of the words for children to unscramble.

◆ Write a recount (link to Literacy) about Trick or Treating.

◆ Design your own spooky costume.

◆ Put the spooky words in alphabetical order.

◆ Design a Halloween poster, and include some spooky Spanish words.

Vocabulario

Spanish	English
el fantasma	a ghost
la calavera	a skull
el disfraz	a costume
el vampiro	a vampire
la casa encantada	a haunted house
la bruja	a witch
los caramelos	sweets
el esqueleto	a skeleton
la araña	a spider
el zombi	a zombie
la calabaza	a pumpkin
truco o trato	trick or treat

Spanish Festivals and Traditions
© Nicolette Hannam, Michelle Williams and Brilliant Publications

Halloween words

el fantasma		la bruja	
la calavera		caramelos	
el disfraz		el esqueleto	
el vampiro		la araña	
la casa encantada		el zombi	

Challenging stereotypes

Background information

Everyone has visual images in their heads of places they have never been to and people they have never met. Even after visiting a country, a full picture may not have been acquired. Stereotypical expectations of Spanish people are that they eat lots of paella! People may think the women all dress as flamenco dancers, and men as matadors. Perhaps a little exaggerated! Stereotypical images of British people are that they wear top hats and tails and speak with posh accents. Stereotypes can be identified for many countries and cultures, and are often very inaccurate.

Stereotypes need to be addressed, discussed, challenged and corrected. It is a subject that can be discussed as part of many lessons, or even after playground fallouts. After discussion, children will conclude that Spanish children are very similar to themselves, with some distinct cultural differences that should be explored and celebrated.

Teaching activities

◆ Class discussion: What is a stereotype? Can you think of any examples?

◆ Discuss children's visual images of a stereotypical Spanish person, and ask them for their reasons/evidence. Use the photocopiable guided sheet on page 79 to compare stereotypical views of Spanish and British people with more realistic views.

◆ Brainstorm other types of stereotypes that exist. Are they positive or negative? Discuss.

◆ Write to an imaginary Spanish child describing daily life in the UK and dispelling any stereotypes.

◆ Look at stereotypes within school, or the local area.

◆ Discuss the features of a stereotypical 'celebrity'. Research people who do not fit this stereotype and who use their fame for positive gain, for example charity work, fighting against injustice.

Challenging stereotypes

Nombre: Fecha:

I recognize that stereotypes are often inaccurate.

Look at the pictures below of stereotypical Spanish and British people. In the boxes underneath draw a more realistic picture of each person, based on the knowledge you have gained in your language lessons.

A stereotypical Spanish person	A stereotypical British person

A realistic Spanish person	A realistic British person

Role models for children

Background information

All children need good role models. Although different in each culture, common themes will remain. Children should be encouraged to look up to authors, sports people and so on. This will help them to become ambitious. It can provide them with real-life reasons to perform and achieve well at school.

Examples of good role models in Britain are David Beckham and J K Rowling. In Spain, children admire Antonio Banderas and Penélope Cruz.

Full name:	José Antonio Domínguez Banderas
Date of birth:	10 August 1960
Place of birth:	Málaga, Andalucía, Spain
Height:	1.74 m

Antonio Banderas wanted to be a professional football player until he broke his foot when he was 14. He then enrolled in drama classes and joined a theatre troupe. His starred in many Spanish films until appearing in his first US film in 1991. At this time he still did not speak any English and learnt his lines phonetically.

He has since appeared in many films, most famously The Mark of Zorro and Spy Kids. In 1999 he became a film director, film producer and singer. He has won three ALMA awards (a tribute to the spirit of pioneering Latinos in television, music, and sports) and been nominated for three Golden Globes.

He is currently married to Melanie Griffiths and they have a daughter.

Full name:	Penélope Cruz Sánchez
Date of birth:	28 April 1978
Place of birth	Alcobendas, Madrid, Spain
Height	1.63 m

Penélope Cruz Sánchez is a Spanish actress, better known as Penélope Cruz. She studied classical ballet for nine years at Spain's National Conservatory and subsequently trained with several prominent dancers.

At fifteen she was discovered when she was chosen at a talent agency audition. She has starred in many Spanish films and several American ones such as 'Vicky Christina Barcelona' and 'Nine'. She has won many awards including a BAFTA for her role in 'Vicky Christina Barcelona' and an Oscar.

Penélope Cruz speaks Spanish, French, Italian and English. In 2007 Penélope and her sister, Mónica, designed a 25 piece clothing collection for the clothes store 'Mango'. She is also a model for 'L'Oréal'.

Teaching activities

◆ Talk about what makes a good role model.

◆ Children could discuss their role models. Who? Why?

◆ Children could draw a picture of their role model and write reasons around it.

◆ Children could draw and research a Spanish role model.

◆ Children could compare a Spanish role model to a British one.

◆ Children could write an acrostic poem using 'Role Model' or the name of their chosen role model.

Alimento español
Spanish food

Background information

Food is an important part of Spanish culture and Spanish people spend a long time preparing food and eating meals. As in other Mediterranean countries, the Spanish diet is considered to be very healthy, including lots of fresh fruit and vegetables, olive oil, garlic and fish.

Breakfast, *el desayuno*, is a quick meal before work or school. Perhaps some bread, *un pan, un cruasán,* or *bollos*. Drinks would include coffee, *un café,* or fruit juice, *zumo*. Lunch, *la comida,* is often eaten late, between 2 and 4pm. Some families still eat lunch together and this is traditionally the largest meal of the day. From 2 – 5pm is a time called *siesta* when people may take a short nap or have a rest! Shops also close.

After school most children have a snack, *merienda,* perhaps a block of chocolate and a glass of milk. After having a large meal at lunchtime, most people prefer to have a lighter supper, *la cena*. Salad, *una ensalada,* and cold meats, *embutidos,* are eaten as late as 10pm. At the weekends, families and friends may gather to eat lengthy lunches, lasting 5 or 6 hours!

Paella

Paella is a traditional Spanish dish and its name comes from the shallow pan which it is cooked in. Paella is made with rice, seafood, chicken, pork or rabbit, peppers, onions, garlic and saffron which gives the rice its deep yellow colour. Paella is traditionally cooked over a wood fire.

Cakes and desserts

Churros are long, thin, sweet, deep fried, doughnut type cakes which are dipped in thick hot chocolate. On Sundays it is tradition for families to go out to a café or bar for these. Rice pudding, *arroz con leche*, is a favourite dessert in Spain.

Drinks

Sherry comes from the Spanish town of Jerez and its surrounding areas. The name for sherry in Spanish is also *jerez*! Sherry comes in four different varieties. *Fino* is dry and pale in colour, *amontillado* is dry with a nutty flavour, *oloroso* is dark in colour with a full flavour and *manzanilla* means chamomile, because it is very pale like chamomile tea.

Sangría is made and drunk all over Spain. It is usually made using red wine, lemonade and fruit.

Soft Sangría (for children)
  $\frac{1}{2}$ cup grape juice/*zumo de uvas*
  $\frac{1}{4}$ cup orange juice/*zumo de naranja*
  $\frac{1}{4}$ to $\frac{1}{2}$ cup Sprite or 7UP (depending on how bubbly you like it)
  Orange slices and other fruits for decorations and to add to drink

Mix ingredients, add ice cubes and serve!

Cava wine is known as the champagne of Spain. It is a fizzy wine produced in Catalonia. The initial wines are blended together and refermented in individual bottles with the addition of a little extra yeast and grape sugar. This second fermentation produces the 'fizz' which is then left for a minimum of 9 months in cool, natural limestone caves. The result is an sparkling wine at affordable prices!

Tapas

Tapas is the name of a variety of appetizers in Spanish cuisine. They can be warm or cold and many different tapas can be combined to make a full meal. The tradition of tapas originates from an old bar custom: people would put bread over their drinks to stop flies going into it. Over time the bread became topped with other foods, such as olives and cheese. Tapas uses ingredients such as olives, spices, tomatoes, peppers, chilies, beans and potatoes. In Spain a lot of seafood is used such as anchovies, prawns and mackerel as well as meats and ham such as *chorizo* sausage.

Teaching activities

◆ Make a menu card for the soft sangría drink labelling the ingredients in Spanish.

◆ Make and taste the soft sangría drink using the recipe on page 81.

◆ Design a tapas menu.

◆ Draw and label typical Spanish food.

◆ Make a list comparing English and Spanish food.

◆ Give children names of food to put in alphabetical order.

◆ Role play being in a café.

◆ Children could learn the names of the shops that food comes from, eg *el pan* (bread) from *la panadería* (the bakery). They could draw the food that is sold in each of the shops on the photocopiable sheet on page 84.

◆ Compare shops in Spain to those in Britain. In both countries many people now shop in large supermarkets to save time.

◆ Compare other buildings and places in a town. Children could draw their local town centre and label it in Spanish.

◆ Link to Maths. Children could use co-ordinates to direct each other around a Spanish town to do their shopping.

◆ Children could design and make a board game based on places in a Spanish town centre.

◆ Children could role play buying items in a shop, first as a whole class and then in small groups or pairs. They could extend their learning by adding size or colour information.

◆ Use a dictionary to translate your school dinner (or packed lunch) today into Spanish.

◆ Bring in some Spanish food for the children to taste.

Vocabulario

el desayuno	breakfast
la comida	lunch
la cena	supper
merienda	snack
el pan	bread
los pasteles	cakes
la panadería	bakers
la pastelería	cake shop
la carnicería	butcher's
el mercado	market
el supermercado	supermarket
la charcutería	deli
la oficina de correos	post office
la farmacia	chemist
la carne	meat
las salchichas	sausages
la fruta	fruit
las verduras	vegetables
el gazpacho	chilled soup
el ajo blanco	white garlic soup
cocido	Spanish stew
tortilla de patatas	Spanish omelette
flan	custard tart
cuajada	set milk pudding
los sellos	stamps

A typical tapas menu

Aceitunas Mixtas – Mixed Spanish Olives
Croquetas de Pollo – Chicken Croquettes
Ensalada Mixta – Mixed Salad
Calamares – Squid
Queso Manchego – Manchego cheese
Patatas Bravas – Fried Potatoes
Gambas a la Plancha – Grilled Prawns
Chorizo – Spicy Sausage
Boquerones – Anchovies in Garlic Oil
Tortilla –Omelette
Tortilla de patatas – Spanish Omelette

Sorbete de Naranja – Orange Sorbet
Tarta de Queso con Chocolate Negro y Blanco
– White and Dark Chocolate Cheesecake

Vino – Wine
Sangría – Sangria
Cerveza – Beer

Spanish food

Nombre: Fecha:

I know where you can buy food in Spain.

Draw the items that can be bought inside each of these shops.

La carnicería

La panadería

El mercado

La pastelería

Now use a dictionary to look up some words for items that might be sold in a supermarket. Carefully write the words in the supermarket trolley.

Spanish Festivals and Traditions
© Nicolette Hannam, Michelle Williams and Brilliant Publications

El Día de Todos los Santos

All Saints day

Background

The 1st November is celebrated throughout the Catholic world as *el Día de Todos los Santos*, or All Saints Day, to honour all the saints. Every day of the year has its own saint or saints, but there are more saints than calendar days, and this one major holy day honors them all. It once was celebrated in May but was moved to offset the paganism of Halloween.

In Spain, the 1st November is a public holiday so shops and banks will be closed. People will use it as a day to visit cemeteries to honour the dead. There is often a Mass, held in the local cemetery, which may include silent processions. People take flowers to the cemeteries.

There are many cemeteries in Spain. The majority of Spaniards are Catholic, most of whom choose burial over cremation. Cemeteries in Spain are well kept and treated with a lot of respect. In Spain this day is a celebration of the lives of those who are no longer with us.

After the visits to the cemetery the day takes on the feel of a fiesta, with a focus on food. People roast chestnuts, *las castañas*, and sweet potatoes, *los boniatos*. In Catalonia, in particular, people would also enjoy almond cakes, *panelletes*.

The play 'Don Juan Tenorio' is always shown on and around this day. It is about the famous Spanish lover. The final scene is set in a cemetery when Don Juan begs the forgiveness of his late lover, Doña Inés.

Teaching activities

◆ Research Catholicism.

◆ Discuss how someone's life can be celebrated.

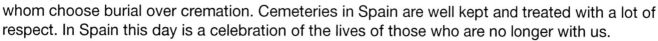

Vocabulario

el cementerio	cemetery
las flores	flowers
las castañas	chestnuts
los boniatos	sweet potatoes
panelletes	almond cakes

Comparing buildings and places

Background information

Spain has a population of over 40 million, with people living in large cities, towns and small villages. In towns and villages generations of families tend to settle and stay living near each other. Tourists tend to visit the famous *costas* for their annual holiday. Spanish towns usually have a market place and a town hall, and a range of large and small shops. Markets are very popular. Main shopping areas are often pedestrianised and, in the warm weather, cafés spread out onto the streets.

Teaching activities

◆ Children could use photocopiable page 87 to draw and label a Spanish town. There is then the opportunity to compare it to the children's home town.

◆ Compare other buildings and places in a town. Children could draw their local town centre and label it in Spanish.

◆ Children could use dictionaries to look up different buildings in their own town, for example, a library.

◆ Link to Maths. Children could use co-ordinates to direct each other around a Spanish town to do their shopping. (See *Vocabulario* box for vocabulary.)

◆ Children could design and make a board game based on places in a Spanish town centre.

◆ Children could role play buying items in a shop, first as a whole class and then in small groups or pairs. They could extend their learning by adding size or colour information.

◆ Give children names of buildings to put in dictionary order.

◆ Can you plan some activities for Spanish children to do in school to teach them about Britain? Who could they learn about? What music could they listen to? Which places should they find on a map? See guided sheet on page 88.

Vocabulario

la panadería	bakers
la pastelería	cake shop
la carnicería	butcher's
el mercado	a market place
el supermercado	supermarket
la charcutería	deli
la oficina de correos	post office
la oficina de turismo	tourist information centre
el banco	bank
el ayuntamiento	town hall
la farmacia	chemist
seguir derecho	straight on
parar	stop
girar a la izquierda	turn left
girar a la derecha	turn right
volver	go back

Spanish Festivals and Traditions
© Nicolette Hannam, Michelle Williams and Brilliant Publications

Comparing buildings and places

Nombre: Fecha:

I can compare buildings in a Spanish town to the buildings in my home town.

Use the words below to draw and label a typical Spanish town and its buildings.
Start with the market place in the middle, and the town hall. Then add some shops
and cafes.

el mercado	market place	la pastelería	cake shop
el ayuntamiento	town hall	la pandería	bakery
la oficina de turismo	Tourist Information Centre	la charcutería	butcher
		el banco	bank
la farmacia	chemists	el supermercado	supermarket

**My Spanish town
Mi Cuidad**

Extension activity
Which buildings are the same in your home town? Which buildings are different?

What I know about Spain

Nombre: Fecha:

I can think about what I already know and what I would like to find out about Spain.

What do you already know about Spain?

What would you like to find out?

How can you find out this information?

What could you tell a Spanish person about your country and your culture?

Extension activity

What activities could Spanish children do in school to help them learn about Britain?

Spanish Festivals and Traditions
© Nicolette Hannam, Michelle Williams and Brilliant Publications

Feliz Navidad
Happy Christmas

Background information
Christmas is a very important festival in Spain and many people go to church during the festive period. Decorations are put up on the 1st December. Nativity scenes, *el belén*, with figurines of Mary, Joseph, Jesus, mule, ox, angel, shepherds and three kings, are laid out on a table at home and life-size figures are also on display in public squares.

Lotería Nacional – 22nd December
The Spanish love the lottery! Every year, just before Christmas, on the 22nd December Spain has the world's biggest state lottery – called *El Gordo* or 'The Fat One'! This is considered to be the start of Christmas Celebrations. People often start buying their tickets as soon as August, and as the 22nd December gets closer, it becomes more difficult to buy your tickets.

La Nochebuena – 24th December
In Spain, the main meal takes place on Christmas Eve, *la Nochebuena*, and consists of a main dish of meat or seafood, such as *cordero*, lamb, *bacalao*, cod, or *marisco*, shellfish. Many families have a traditional meal, *pavo trufado de Navidad* which is roast turkey and truffles. After the meal families may gather round the tree and sing carols. This is the most important family gathering of the year. The meal may be interrupted, at midnight, by the ringing of the bells calling families to Mass.

In Spain, it is tradition to eat sweets at Christmas. *El turrón*, nougat, is essential. This almond-based sweet traditionally comes in a block and there are two types, *duro*, hard, with whole almonds in a paste of sugar, honey and egg white, or *blando*, soft, where the ingredients are mixed together. Marzipan figures, *las figuras de mazapán*, are also popular.

El día de los Santos Inocentes – 28th December
The equivalent of April's Fools Day takes place in Spain on the 28th December, *el día de los Santos Inocentes*, Holy Innocents' day.

La Nochevieja (New Year's Eve) – 31st December
On New Year's Eve, *la Nochevieja*, it is tradition to participate in a celebration called, the 'lucky grapes', *las uvas de la suerte*. On each stroke of midnight you take a grape and make a wish for the New Year ahead, *el Año Nuevo*. Other superstitions include wearing something red and putting gold in the champagne for good luck. New Year's Eve is a big celebration in Spain with many street parties. The 1st January is a public holiday.

El Día de los Reyes – 6th January
Spanish tradition has it that the Three Kings, *los Reyes Magos*, are the ones who, on the morning of the 6th January, *el Día de los Reyes*, bring presents for all the children. Some families have decided to switch to *Papá Noel* on Christmas Day, as in other countries. A large family meal at lunchtime is common, as is a visit to church.

Teaching activities

◆ Children could taste some traditional Spanish Christmas food and wish each other *Feliz Navidad*

◆ Use a dictionary to translate some of the food we eat at Christmas.

◆ Listen to some traditional Christmas carols in both languages and compare.

◆ Children could copy a short carol out in their best handwriting and decorate it for display. Use page 91 as support.

◆ Children could write a letter to *Papá Noel* using the frame on the photocopiable sheet (page 92).

Vocabulario	
Feliz Navidad	Happy Christmas
Nochebuena	24th December
Navidad	25th December
Noche Vieja	31st December
Papá Noel	Father Christmas
el árbol de Navidad	Christmas tree
la comida de Navidad	Christmas dinner
los regalos	presents
los Reyes Magos	The Three Kings
la estrella	the star
el establo	the stable

Vocabulary for the letter	
Querido Papá Noel	Dear Father Christmas
Me gustaría	I would like …
Por favor	Please
Gracias	Thank you very much

◆ Draw and label a nativity scene in Spanish.

◆ Children could dress up as nativity characters and try a brief role-play in Spanish using simple greetings and questions.

◆ Draw and label a Christmas tree. Describe the colours in Spanish.

◆ Children could draw and label some presents they would like to receive. They could also draw and label some presents they would like to give to family members.

◆ Children could draw and label a traditional Spanish Christmas dinner.

◆ Use photocopiable sheet page 93 to compare English and Spanish Christmas celebrations in the form of a Venn diagram.

◆ Make Spanish Christmas cards.

Christmas carols

Comparison of the Spanish and English words and their meanings could lead into a discussion about Christmas celebrations in different countries.

'Noche de Paz' - 'Silent Night'

Noche de paz,
noche de fe.

El portal de Belén
vibra en cánticos llenos de amor
dulces cánticos al Redentor
que esta noche nació
y es más hermoso que el sol.

Noche de paz,
noche de amor.

Despertar que en Belén
de María un rosal floreció
y el portal se ilumina en su honor
adorar al señor
porque es el hijo de Dios.

Noche de paz,
noche de fe.

Al portal de Belén
los arcángeles llegan también
van cantando alabanzas a Dios
todo el mundo a sus pies
hoy ha nacido el Señor

Feliz Navidad

Nombre: Fecha:

I can write a short letter to Papá Noel.

Spanish Festivals and Traditions
© Nicolette Hannam, Michelle Williams and Brilliant Publications

Feliz Navidad

Nombre: Fecha:

I can compare Christmas and New Year traditions in the United Kingdom and Spain.

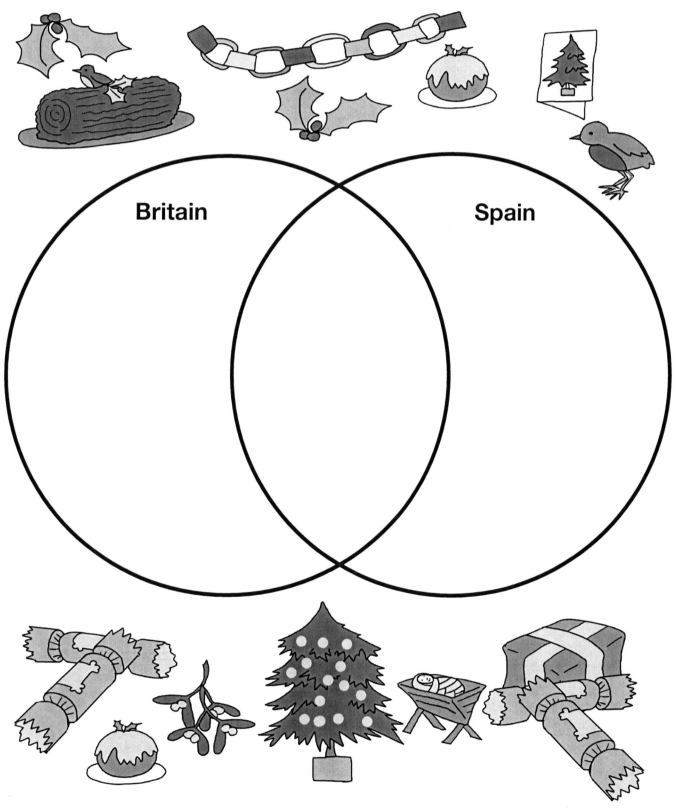

Planning a Spanish Day for your school

A Spanish Day can help to raise the profile of Modern Foreign Languages and give staff and children the chance to enjoy the language as a large group. You can celebrate previous successes and enthuse pupils about future learning. To give the day a bigger impact, staff and children can be asked to wear red and yellow – the colours of the Spanish flag.

When organizing the day, we recommend you provide teachers with all the resources they will need, to help alleviate stress and to allow them to participate fully in the day and enjoy themselves. On the following pages you will find lesson plans and photocopiable resources for the following four tried and tested activities:

Activity A – Pablo Picasso
Art – Learning about the Spanish artist Picasso and drawing a self portrait in his style.

Activity B – Spanish food
Food tasting and making a place mat.

Activity C – Parachute activities and learning a song
Parachute activities following Spanish instructions.
Learn a song and some actions for everyone to perform together in the final assembly.

Activity D – Classroom activity
Playing board games using Spanish language.

We recommend having two assemblies: one in the morning to explain what will happen and set the tone for the day, and one at the end, so that you can celebrate your achievements. Here is a possible timetable:

Class		Session 1		Session 2		Session 3	Session 4	
1	Registration	Classroom activity	Assembly – sing some songs children have already learned. Explanation of day's activities	Parachute, then song	Playtime	Art	Food tasting	Dinnertime
2		Classroom activity		Song, then parachute		Food tasting	Art	
3		Art		Food tasting		Parachute, then song	Classroom activity	
4		Food tasting		Art		Song, then parachute	Classroom activity	
5		Art		Food tasting		Classroom activity	Parachute, then song	
6		Food tasting		Art		Classroom activity	Song, then parachute	
7		Parachute, then song		Classroom activity		Food tasting	Art	
8		Song, then parachute		Classroom activity		Art	Food tasting	

The pupil evaluation sheet on pages 103–104 can be used to reinforce intercultural understanding and will help you to develop ideas further.

Spanish Festivals and Traditions
© Nicolette Hannam, Michelle Williams and Brilliant Publications

Activity A - Pablo Picasso

Objectives
◆ To learn about Pablo Picasso
◆ To draw a self-portrait in his style

Background information
◆ Pablo Picasso was born in 1881 in Málaga, Spain.
◆ His full name is Pablo Diego José Francisco de Paula Juan Nepomuceno María de los Remedios Cipriano de la Santísima Trinidad Ruiz y Picasso. It is a name that honours saints and relatives. The names Ruiz and Picasso are added for his mum and dad, as is tradition in Spain.
◆ He had four children in total.
◆ He is most famous for his work and influence on the Cubist movement. It is the idea that an object should be shown from multiple points of view simultaneously.
◆ Picasso also worked in ceramics, drawing, sculpture and printmaking.
◆ He died in 1973 in France.

Resources provided by MFL Coordinator
• Example of Pablo Picasso's 1907 self-portrait painting.
• Some questions in Spanish for teachers to ask about the original piece of work.

Class teacher will need to provide
• Paper for children to paint on
• Selection of paints and painting equipment

Teaching activities
◆ Look at Pablo Picasso's self-portrait painting (this can be found on the Internet) and print copies off or use it on an Interactive Whiteboard. Discuss the painting with the children, explaining that Picasso has used oil on canvas to paint this self portrait. It is mask like, and influenced by African art.

◆ Explain that you would like the children to produce a self portrait in the style of Picasso's painting. Summarise the key features they will need to include. Explain the resources and time they have available.

◆ At the end of the session you could ask children to talk about the colours of their painting in Spanish. You could evaluate the paintings and summarise how and why they are in the style of Picasso.

Activity B – Spanish food

Objectives

◆ To taste some Spanish food
◆ To know how to ask for the food in Spanish
◆ To know the Spanish names of some fruit and vegetables
◆ To make a place mat

Teaching activities

◆ Prepare some Spanish food for the children to taste. Encourage them to ask for it in Spanish (see below).

◆ Before tasting the food teach the names of fruit and vegetables in Spanish.

◆ Explain the phrases 'Me gusta' for 'I like' and 'No me gusta' for 'I don't like' so that children can complete them on their place mats. Also teach the following:

Me gustaría …	I would like …
Por favor	Please
Gracias	Thank you

◆ Then provide each child with a place mat frame to decorate during the lesson, together with laminated copies of the sheets of fruits and vegetables (one per table). The place mats can later be laminated and sent home.

◆ Whilst the children work, take around the food for them to try. Play some Spanish café music, if you have a CD, to help to pretend that you really are in Spain!

◆ What could children ask for and how?

Me gustaría pan y queso por favor.　　　I would like some bread and cheese, please.

Me gustaría un pastel por favor.　　　I would like some cake, please.

Me gustaría chorizo por favor.　　　I would like some chorizo sausage please

Me gustaría zumo de naranja por favor.　　　I would like some orange juice, please.

Me gustaría chocolate caliente por favor.　　　I would like a hot chocolate, please.

◆ Encourage them to say thank you (*Gracias*).

Spanish Festivals and Traditions
© Nicolette Hannam, Michelle Williams and Brilliant Publications

Frutas

una manzana

una pera

unas fresas

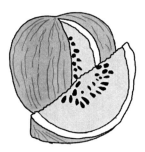

un melón

unas cerezas

un melocotón

una toronja

un plátano

una piña

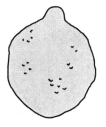

un limón

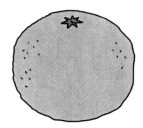

una naranja

unas uvas

Verdura

una cebolla

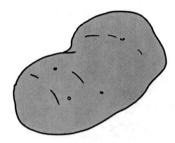

una patata

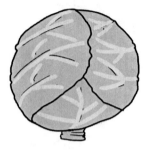

una col

un champiñón

unos guisantes

unas zanahorias

un pepino

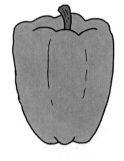

un pimiento

un brécol

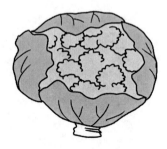

una coliflor

una berenjena

un maíz

No me gusta

Me gusta

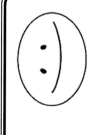

Activity C – Parachute games and a song to learn

Objectives
◆ To participate in some Spanish-themed parachute games
◆ To learn a song and some actions to sing with everyone in the assembly at the end of the day

Resources provided by MFL Coordinator
• Parachute
• A laminated copy of this sheet
• CD and song sheet for chosen song – there are some Spanish song books with CDs to choose from. One recommendation is: a song from Vamos a Cantar.
• CD player

Teaching activities
◆ There are two activities to complete this session. Each class needs time in the hall or the playground to try some parachute games. Start with teaching the children simple instructions in Spanish:

A la izquierda	Left
A la derecha	Right
Pasear	Walk
Parar	Stop
Más rápido	Faster
Más lento	Slower
Levantar	Lift
Más bajo	Lower

◆ Then teach the following games. Call out instructions in Spanish.

Número (numbers)
Give each child a number from 1–5: *uno, dos, tres, cuatro, cinco*. When you call out a number, those children run round to a new place.

Gato y ratón (cat and mouse)
Everyone holds the parachute stretched out at about waist height. Someone becomes a mouse and goes underneath. Someone else becomes a cat and goes on top. The rest of the group try to hide the mouse by moving the parachute up and down.

Champiñón (mushroom)
Can you all reach parachute above your heads, pull it down behind you and sit down with it under your bottom to form a mushroom shape? Once inside your mushroom you could count around the circle in Spanish, name colours, etc.

◆ Back in class pupils can listen to a song and learn the words. It is even more fun if everyone learns the same actions as well. The song can be performed as a very large group in assembly.

Activity D – Classroom activity

Objective
◆ To use Spanish vocabulary when playing co-operatively

Teaching activities
◆ This activity consists of a selection of games the children can choose to play in pairs or small groups.

◆ Give each pair or group a laminated card of vocabulary to help them use some Spanish.

Resources provided by MFL Coordinator
• Suggested games: Snakes and Ladders, Ludo, Snap or Dominoes. There are many resources available as images on the Internet that can be colour printed and laminated (for example, Snakes and Ladders boards)
• Laminated cards to support vocabulary (page 102)

Class teacher will need to provide
• Colouring pencils
• Scissors
• Dice
• Counters

How to play games in Spanish

◆ Choose a game to play with a friend or in a small group.

◆ Try to use some Spanish language. Here are some useful phrases:

¿Te gustaría jugar?	Would you like to play?
Te toca	Your turn
Me toca	My turn
Tú ganas	You win
Yo gano	I win

◆ Say the number on the dice aloud.

◆ Count in Spanish as you move along the board:

uno	one
dos	two
tres	three
cuatro	four
cinco	five
seis	six
siete	seven
ocho	eight
nueve	nine
diez	ten
once	eleven
doce	twelve

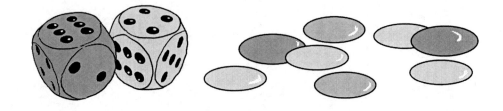

Spanish Festivals and Traditions
© Nicolette Hannam, Michelle Williams and Brilliant Publications

Spanish Day

Nombre: Fecha:

I have participated in our Spanish Day.

Draw and describe the activities that took place in the box below.

Which activities did you enjoy? Explain why.

What did you learn?

Ask a friend what they enjoyed most and why.

Which activities would you plan for Spanish children whose school was having an English day?

Spanish Festivals and Traditions
© Nicolette Hannam, Michelle Williams and Brilliant Publications

Useful resources

Resource books published by Brilliant Publications

¡Vamos a Cantar!
¡Es Español!
Spanish Pen Pals made Easy
Lotto en Español
Juguemos Todos Juntos
Buena Idea